T0147160

RIDING THE WAVE OF CHANGE

Hope, Healing and Spiritual Growth for Our World

E V E   W I L S O N

BALBOA.
PRESS

A DIVISION OF HAY HOUSE

Copyright © 2017 Eve Wilson.

All rights reserved. No part of this book may be used or reproduced by any means, graphic, electronic, or mechanical, including photocopying, recording, taping or by any information storage retrieval system without the written permission of the author except in the case of brief quotations embodied in critical articles and reviews.

Balboa Press books may be ordered through booksellers or by contacting:

Balboa Press
A Division of Hay House
1663 Liberty Drive
Bloomington, IN 47403
www.balboapress.com
1 (877) 407-4847

Because of the dynamic nature of the Internet, any web addresses or links contained in this book may have changed since publication and may no longer be valid. The views expressed in this work are solely those of the author and do not necessarily reflect the views of the publisher, and the publisher hereby disclaims any responsibility for them.

The author of this book does not dispense medical advice or prescribe the use of any technique as a form of treatment for physical, emotional, or medical problems without the advice of a physician, either directly or indirectly. The intent of the author is only to offer information of a general nature to help you in your quest for emotional and spiritual well-being. In the event you use any of the information in this book for yourself, which is your constitutional right, the author and the publisher assume no responsibility for your actions.

Any people depicted in stock imagery provided by Thinkstock are models, and such images are being used for illustrative purposes only. Certain stock imagery © Thinkstock.

Print information available on the last page.

ISBN: 978-1-5043-5661-9 (sc)
ISBN: 978-1-5043-5660-2 (hc)
ISBN: 978-1-5043-5662-6 (e)

Library of Congress Control Number: 2016906580

Balboa Press rev. date: 08/11/2017

Contents

Part I: Sunlight Warms Water and Earth............................ 1

You Are Ascending 3

Memory: A Tremendous Gift 6

Hope, Confidence, Wisdom, and Skill........................... 11

The Essence of Truth 12

Finding True Satisfaction 14

Part II: Wind on the Water... 17

Qabalah – The Tree of Life... 19

The Path of the Lightning Bolt 22

A Brief Overview of the Tree of Life..........................23

The Healing Qabalah..29

Kether – Above the Head – The One Source 30

Chokmah – Right Side of Head – Remember..............32

Memory – A Chokmah Experience 33

Two Visions and a Miracle...35

Vision 1 from Chokmah: Looking into Binah.............37

Vision 2 from Chokmah: The Creation of

Conflict and Opposition...39

Vision 2 from Chokmah – Part B: The Forces

of Creation and Death and Their Resolution

in the New World...40

Binah – Left Side of Head – Cosmic Womb 42

Daat – Back of Throat – God has left us here alone 45

Chesed– Right Shoulder– Incarnating.................................... 47

Geburah – Left Shoulder – Breaking Through........................ 49

    Allegory 51

Tipheret – Center Torso – Unity, God Within 54

    A True Story of Choices.. 57

Netzach – Right Hip – The Force of Nature 62

Hod – Left Hip – The Mind, Focus, Follow-Through 66

    Memory – Osprey 67

Yesod– Reproductive Area – Contracts 70

    Soul Contracts 70

    Mind Over Matter... 73

Malkuth – Under Foot – The Physical World, Earth 76

    Vision – Mother Earth – 2010 79

Part III: Waves of Change 81

Hitting the Bottom of the Tree 83

Enlightened Souls within Our Seas 87

Death and Rebirth... 97

    Vision of Redwood Tree 1... 99

    Redwood Tree, Meditation 1.. 99

    Redwood Tree, Meditation 2.. 100

    Dream.. 101

    Vision of Redwood Tree 2... 101

    Endings and Beginnings 102

    Letting Go of Baggage 104

    Where We Have Been Broken.. 106

The End of Sorrow – Ascension.. 107

    The Future.. 108

    Steps to Ascension – Chakra Awakenings..................... 111

Part IV: Surfing 117

    Tools to Streamline Ascension 119

    Owning Your Authority in Life........................142

Closing Thoughts 149

Acknowledgments.. 151

Glossary of Terms 153

About the Author 173

Waves ~
Sunlight warms water and earth, generating wind
Wind on the water stimulates the water and creates waves
Waves challenge us, creating change and opportunities for growth
Surfing—riding the waves of change

Part I

SUNLIGHT WARMS WATER AND EARTH

I sense that I must find the strength
To shape my soul in worthy fashion
To form herself as spirit's garment

– Rudolf Steiner, *the Calendar of the Soul*

You Are Ascending

You are evolving in ways that have been preordained since the beginning of time. Beneath the challenging and often negative aspects of life, there is something marvelous and purposeful going on. This book will help you to orient toward the positive shifts taking place, so you can ride the wave of change on planet Earth with confidence and grace.

The evolution of life we are experiencing now is as significant for life on Earth as when the first land creatures emerged from the primordial swamp. Beneath the apparently negative evolutionary indicators of our present age—which include global warming, overpopulation, limited resources, and damage to the environment due to human technology—there is a true evolution of soul. This deeper evolution has always been the underlying reason for life. This book is about that positive aspect of evolution for planet and soul, which is called *ascension*. Ascension is the journey by which we emerge from the swamp of our lower energies of hatred, fear, and destructive behavior and evolve into our true potential of union with our own higher intelligence, purpose, and love.

There are two directions of evolution relevant to this book, which we call the *old world* and the *new world.* The old world has been our experience since the beginning of time, only recently nearing the fulfillment of its purpose on earth. It is a journey of separation from our spiritual root in the oneness of all things. Its purpose has been the development of independent vehicles: souls to carry our spirit, life forms to carry our souls, and planets for us to live and evolve within. This separation from our original state of oneness and unconditional love was necessary to create many life forms with individuality and independence out of the state of absolute oneness of spirit. This part of our journey caused a great deal of suffering, and we can be grateful that this direction has pretty much done its job and is on its way out, so we can get on with the more enjoyable phases to come.

The new world is the intended goal for all that has gone before, and it began to slowly awaken within our collective human souls as early as the mid-1800s. Its goal is to take the raw forms of life as we know them and bring them into a more refined state capable of growing with sustained intelligence and love. The new world emerges as we reengage our independent souls, bodies, and planet with our root in the oneness of spirit from which all life was conceived. Yet we retain the uniqueness and individuality we have developed during the old-world experience. Ascension is the raising of vibration within all of life, which brings us into range for receiving our true spiritual selves into the independent souls, bodies, and planet our true selves have created. By ascending, all life forms will eventually become suitable homes for the intelligence and love that characterize us at the level of our eternal spiritual root in the state of oneness.

Rudolf Steiner, who lived from the mid-1800s through the early 1900s, stimulated the evolution of soul in many fields of human endeavor, from spirituality to science, and art to education. I see him as planting seeds of ascension that continue to influence us today. His visionary work included the founding of Waldorf schools, which are now among the fastest-growing alternative school systems in the world. The underlying intent of Waldorf education is remarkable in its uniqueness. Steiner observed that small children live in close relationship with the angelic realms of spirit but gradually lose that connection as they mature and grow more deeply engaged with their physical bodies. The intention of Waldorf education is to assist the soul in maintaining its spiritual connections while developing its human qualities of imagination and independent thought. This method nurtures the awakening of the innate genius within each person. Here was a man who clearly understood the true purpose of life on earth. I gratefully share his profound and unique thinking in quotes provided throughout this book. They are all excerpted from his book *Calendar of the Soul*, a guide through the weeks of the year that encourages us to grow our souls in response to the spiritual influences of the seasons.

The Mayans knew about the end of the old world and predicted it with the end of the Mayan calendar in December 2012. What we experienced was, fortunately, not the end of the world as some people feared as that time approached, but the end of the old-world soul contracts that predominantly defined our experience prior to that date (see *soul contracts*, Glossary of Terms). Since then, we have been moving with increasing confidence and strength into the new world and a whole new set of contracts.

While the old contracts have ended, it will take time for the work they have initiated to finish. There is a continuum of change: the old world lingers, getting less and less potent, and the new world strengthens, its goals and contracts increasingly becoming the norm. The transition from the old to the new can sometimes be intense, rather like cold and warm fronts meeting and creating storms. But a lot of the distress can be weathered more easily by simply choosing to focus your life within the new world and not fighting with the old. It is like stepping through a doorway into a calmer place. You can always step back the other way as well, out of habit or in response to an event or incident. This book will help you to choose the new world and to grow stronger in that experience, so you can ride these changes with ease and grace.

So let us learn to ride these waves of change together! But first some background about me and how I came to be writing this book, teaching, healing, and working with personal and planetary ascension.

Please take advantage of the Glossary of Terms at the end of this book. It will clarify the words I use and what I intend to express in employing them. My use of spiritual terms may differ significantly from the way you have seen them used before.

Memory: A Tremendous Gift

It's a quiet morning in 1986. I'm standing in the healing space in my home, where I offer healing treatments for a living now, as instructed during a conversation with God earlier in the year.

Contemplating my poster of the Kabbalistic Tree of Life by Patricia Waldygo, I sense a presence and turn to see a being of beautiful golden light standing to my right. The feeling is of purity and strength. I immediately realize it is Archangel Michael, although I have no recollection of having met him before; there is no mistaking his identity. There is joy, comfort, and safety in his presence, and he has my rapt attention.

With my inner ear, heart, and belly, I clearly perceive that he is offering to teach me the Qabalah as a healing tool. I happily agree and then feel an inner shift by which I receive a holographic awareness of the Healing Qabalah as a way of working with the Tree of Life. It is amazingly straightforward, clear, and practical in its application, and I feel that I can immediately apply its wisdom and gifts.

> *Archangel Michael, how can I ever thank you enough for this amazing gift that is a foundation for all of my work? And how can I express my appreciation for all the years of comfort, protection, and support you have given me? Perhaps I may begin to show my gratitude by sharing this gift, not only with my clients and students but also in this book.*

From the start of my healing practice, as I sought to understand and help those who came to me for healing, my direct connection with God led me to angels and spiritual beings of unconditional love who helped me open to my higher self. They reassured me that I would know what was needed when I listened to the wisdom within me. They guided me to look beyond my assumptions to see the deeper cause of disease. I learned that my job was to bring people to the place where they were open and ready to be healed, not only at the conscious level but also at the deep level of cause where disease begins. Once there, the intelligence and energy of unconditional love and truth—either directly from the Source, or through archangels and ascended master healers—could support the innate intelligence and wisdom within my clients to correct their imbalances and bring healing. The process of feeling my way through each healing led me to greater levels of discernment and self-awareness, which allowed me to become a better healer. Over time, I increasingly came to see the way that each person's story is a microcosm of the greater unfolding evolution of life.

Gradually, through many years and innumerable experiences of healing, I began to understand the deeper significance beneath the challenges we experience. I now see a greater portion of the spiritual purpose behind our experiences of life and look forward to sharing it with you in this book. My perspective increases with each passing day, so even though I can share with you only a partial understanding, I feel that it can be a true foundation to assist your innate wisdom and spirit to guide you in the fulfillment of your own unique purpose in life. It is my calling to put these words on paper for you, and so I will trust that what I offer here will be helpful to you.

Through the journey of ascension, we are each coming to increasingly know our true nature. We gradually become aware that we are, and have always been, exactly who and what life needed us to be. We are each unique and essential at every stage of our growth and evolution.

My job as an author and healer is to open people to the remembrance of their own value and of the benevolence of life. Healing requires bringing kindness, love, and respect to the darker places within people's souls and our world, allowing those places to remember the truth that is always present at their core. A tiny opening to that unconditionally loving truth initiates healing of hurt, anger, blame, and despair. Then, when we are ready, forgiveness and love can begin to clear the negative states and restore hope and a willingness to live and continue to grow to a body, a soul, a society, or the world.

Hope is an essential seed of ascension. It is gentle, but has vast power. Like a tiny trickle of water can wash away a wall, it gradually sets free those places within us that have been stuck in dark states of consciousness and allows the light of our true nature to shine through.

I have great hope for our future, not based on wishful thinking, but built on decades of observing how people can heal from the darkest places and discover that everything in life has a purpose and gift that is vastly greater than the suffering. I have seen this in individuals, families, and soul groups. I have seen the way these smaller works of love influence and often protect us in individual lives, our country, and our world, despite the darkness of fear and greed that appear so vast.

Much of what we see happening to the physical planet, and what appears to be death and destruction, is an opportunity for change and growth. Be open to unexpected miracles, and don't limit your assumptions about our future by the despair of our past. As more and more souls awaken to their oneness with Source and all beings, life will rally on every level, although it may look pretty nasty at different points along the way. Welcome a spirit of hope to live within your heart and mind despite appearances.

I see amazing shifts happening on the spiritual planes of our world, which are the foundational energies that birth what happens in the physical realm. There is an increasing presence of light, peace, truth, and wholeness. Higher levels of consciousness are being born and coming into position to change the path of our evolution on Earth. These changes are happening exponentially in the spiritual aura of our planet, and the powers of love and truth are on the ascension. The physical world has no choice but to follow, more slowly, but inevitably, to reflect in form the changes that are happening in spirit.

I am excited to share with you some of the vast perspective I have gained through my work and to pass on to you a vision that may help liberate your soul to ascend smoothly into increasing union with your true self! The presence of hope within you is an open door for healing to occur not only for you but also for those you love and for the Earth!

To carry Spirit's light to world-winter night
Strives blissfully the impulse of my heart,
That shining seeds of soul
Take root in grounds of worlds,
And Word of God in senses' darkness
Resounds, transfiguring all being

—Rudolf Steiner, *the Calendar of the Soul*

Hope, Confidence, Wisdom, and Skill

We on planet Earth are experiencing a transformation called ascension. I will explain this transition and how it moves us in the direction of realizing our true purpose and potential for life. I intend to impart hope and confidence as well as wisdom and tools to support you during this change, helping you to ride the wave of change with grace.

The first thing I'd like to share is a clearer perspective on life's true intention, both for the experiences we have undergone in the past and the promise inherent in our future. I will begin with the story of our evolution, using the Qabalah, which is a glyph that functions as a foundational template for life. As I introduce you to this wonderful tool, I'll help you find new meaning and value in our individual and collective past.

Then I'll return to the present day, making a 180-degree turn in the direction of our evolution. I'll explore what it means for us that the process of ascension is accelerating and how it will lead us back into unity with our higher truth, each other, and all life forms.

Most importantly, I will help you to own your own Inner Wisdom and truth and learn to guide your life from that true inner compass, gaining strength and self-mastery.

Finally, I will introduce you to the Archangels—life's loving managers who coordinate the many levels of intelligence and unconditional love that create our reality. They will provide unconditionally loving support as you raise your vibration on every level of body, emotion, mind, spirit, soul, and experience. In Part IV, Tools to Streamline Ascension, I'll teach you to access their help and give you tools to streamline your journey of ascension. Through the ascension process, you will grow to fulfill the promise innate within you. These tools will help prepare you to find truth and fulfillment (at last!) within the new world experience as it emerges here on Earth.

The Essence of Truth

Being spiritual but not religious, I find it a challenge to choose words to express what I want to share with you. So many spiritual words and terms are steeped in contexts I don't want to align with. Recreating the language altogether to have a pure spiritual set of terms requires too much work, and so I gave up trying long ago. I would like to explain some important terms I will use and what exactly I mean by them, so you can interpret my meaning as I intend. The Glossary of Terms at the end of the book provides further clarification.

A long time ago, a very dear teacher of mine, Grandmother Twyla Nitch of the Iroquois Nation, taught me a term that has been very helpful on my journey. She called the Higher Power by the name *Great Mystery* and described it as present within all of life. When I said to her that I found people mysterious, but didn't find that One mysterious, she suggested I use the term the Essence of Truth.

The Essence of Truth to me is the purest, truest focus of spirit available to me at a given moment. I feel this term can be used when seeking that truth within one's self—the Essence of Truth within me. Or for accessing that truth that is often called God without getting caught in religious interpretations—the Essence of Truth of God. Or to identify and access the true focus of any aspect of life that you would want, including your angels and spirit guides—the Essence of Truth of Archangel Michael, for instance. There are many levels of consciousness present within the complex nature of a person at any given time. So using this term helps you to access your wisest, truest self and that of the spiritual energies you seek to partner with.

God is a term that is convenient, and I use it because it is generally understood in our culture to mean our highest focus of spiritual truth and Oneness. However, this term has been used in many conflictual ways throughout history and has often been a focus for abuses supposedly carried out "in the name of God." When I use the term God, I am speaking of the Essence of Truth of God, not a lower interpretation of that name. I believe the Essence of Truth of God is both the source of life and present within all of life, although often hidden beneath a sort of slumber or forgetfulness that we experience in the old world state. The ascension process awakens that slumbering truth gradually, recalling us to our higher nature, which is the Essence of Truth of our own unique facet of God within human form. The same awakening occurs in nature and the planet as they ascend, too.

Having said this, with words commonly used in religious connotations, I will alternate terms to prevent people from habitually inserting a religious meaning over what I am trying to communicate as a spiritual experience. For example, in addition to the Essence of Truth of God, I also will use the One, the Source, and the One Source. For those who don't believe in a higher power, this may seem to be cutting the distinction pretty thin. Bear with me; I hope my meaning will come through clearly as you read. Please feel free to insert, where needed, the words that resonate more truly with you.

Finding True Satisfaction

Within each living soul there is a deeper place that longs to be filled. This longing calls, pulls, and tugs us in all kinds of directions, seeking satisfaction from outside of us, but what we need is already present within our own selves and can only be found within us.

A seed of longing is planted within to compel us through life experiences to learn and grow in ways we would miss if we were not dissatisfied. Through this process we will all eventually come to realize that satisfaction gained from outside of ourselves is very temporary. It may arrive in a moment and be gone just as quickly, leaving us with its memory and an even deeper longing to be fulfilled.

Once we reach the awareness that satisfaction from an outside source is illusory, where do we go from there? Within us is the very thing we desire most, and the drive toward satisfaction, when turned inward toward the true core of our beings, will ultimately guide us to discover it. But in order to have this precious inner gift, we need to stop trying to fill the hole in our souls with temporary or illusory things. Outer satisfactions are good, but they are the icing on the cake, they are not the cake. **You are the satisfaction you seek.**

You are more than your body, emotions, and mind; **you are an eternal focus of spiritual being, a presence of truth and unconditional love**. You have been building a soul through all of your incarnations, creating it as a vehicle to carry you deeper and deeper into the world. While up until now you have been mostly outside of your soul, you have guided it through challenges that would develop it into the perfect vehicle for your true self to live within. Your soul is your spiritual vehicle, and it lives within the physical vehicle of your body. Through all of your lifetimes, you have been developing soul muscles, strengths, gifts, and potentials that would make your soul a suitable place for your eternal spirit to inhabit. This is the lifetime where the eternal spirit that you are is beginning to awaken within your soul and body to actualize yourself within the world. **It is time for the true you to be here!**

It is the state of unity between body, soul, and divine-eternal self that will satisfy you. Until now, food, mood-altering substances, success, and relationships were as close as you could come, but they are temporary satisfactions at best. Realizing this, many follow a religion, a spiritual path, or spend time in nature; any of these can be a step in the right direction for them. However, sooner or later, you have to take the leap of faith and own the potential within your own soul for yourself.

It is as though you have a gorgeous sports car sitting in your driveway, but you don't know how to drive it, so you keep giving the keys to other people: doctors, spiritual leaders, psychologists, parents, friends, or lovers. But no one can drive your body and soul successfully except for you. No one can tell you how to drive it, because each person's soul is unique. People can talk about their own journeys and experiences, which may inspire you. However, reading someone else's driver's manual won't tell you how to drive your own vehicle. You are its creator, and you need to master it for yourself.

This might sound odd, because I make my living healing and teaching spiritually. It is what I am good at and what my soul is designed to do. But I am also dedicated to leading people toward the mastery of their own souls.

How do you master your soul? As the process of ascension continues in your life, mastery will increasingly become your natural state. In the meantime, you can practice accessing your inner truth and living from that place of increasing personal authority.

Within your heart chakra—in the middle of your chest, but back at its core just behind your spine—there is a place of deep peace and balance that is a natural home to your own essence of truth, the eternal spark of the divine that you are. I call this your *Inner Wisdom*, and it can be found anywhere within you, but it is most awake in your heart chakra. In Part IV of this book you'll find detailed instructions for accessing and using your Inner Wisdom and increasing it through using balance points.

Part II

WIND ON THE WATER

The Foundation for Creation

Qabalah – The Tree of Life

From the smallest particle to the largest universe, every life form has its own foundational structure called a Qabalah or Tree of Life.

Composed of ten spheres, the Qabalah is the structure upon which God, the One, the All That Is, created life.

Early in my journey as a healer, Archangel Michael gave me the Healing Qabalah, a very practical application of what has traditionally been a very esoteric system. It has been an anchor point for me, helping me understand human life, our world, and our universe. This understanding allows me to bring healing across time and space and through all lifetimes to the place and time where it will have the greatest beneficial impact on a soul's evolution and wholeness. It also directs me as to how I may best assist in the ascension process. Thank you, Archangel Michael!

If you are a student of Kabbalah/Qabalah, please approach this work with an open mind and heart. What I share here is built upon years of personal experience using it as a healing tool. My interpretations of the spheres are necessarily subjective to the journey of my work. I believe this is why the Qabalah is given to us as a glyph, rather than a book; everyone who needs it can access the elements required for their present work. Representing all of creation, the Qabalah reveals much that has never before been written or taught, even in the many books and traditions that contain its wisdom. The aspects of each sphere on the Tree of Life that I am focusing on for the purposes of this book are specific to these lessons and not intended to explain all of what each sphere can represent in its entirety. I hope you will find that what I share has a helpful application to your life's journey. More importantly, I hope your own meditations on the Qabalah will provide you with the inspiration and wisdom you need to take the next step on your own path of evolution.

Whether you are new to the Qabalah or an experienced student of it, I offer it as a practical tool, the way that Archangel Michael taught it to me. I will use it in this book as a foundation for understanding our journey through life up to this point and to help guide you through the ascension process.

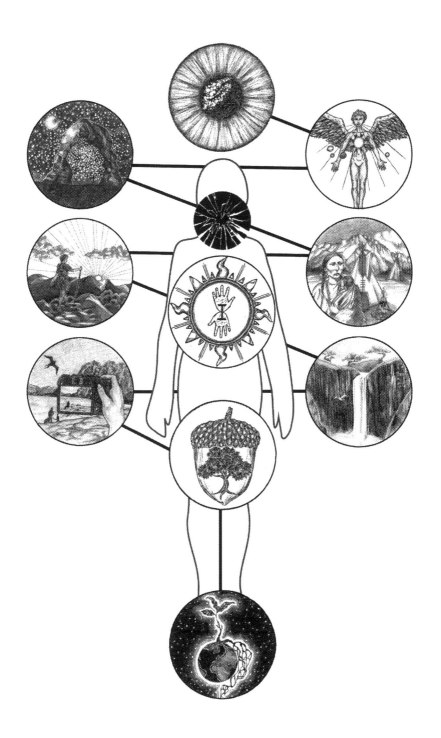

The Path of the Lightning Bolt
Evolution of Soul and Form

Flowing from the top of the Tree of Life down through its spheres in a zigzag manner is the journey of evolution (see the Qabalah diagram). Here we may come to understand the influence of the Source of life acting as Creator, giving birth to the souls, worlds, and bodies that will someday be ready to truly express the love and intentions of that One in many forms. Throughout time and all of our incarnations, the Creator has been working to build the qualities and capacities that will be needed for the future union of higher spiritual consciousness with each individual and each type of life form. This evolutionary journey of souls, as seen on the Tree of Life, is called the Path of the Lightning Bolt.

However, life is not really linear. It is holographic, which is much harder to describe. There is a complete Tree of Life within every sphere on the Tree, and the phases of evolution represented on the Tree of Life repeat endlessly, in different ways within us and the world. If you've ever sat in a room where there are mirrors on both sides of you, you can see the room repeating over and over in each direction. Life is like that, more prismatic than linear; so while we follow the two-dimensional idea of the Path of the Lightning Bolt, I will use the languages of dream and vision, in addition to linear ideas, to awaken soul memory and deeper understanding.

Each sphere on your personal Qabalah corresponds with a part of your physical body. The Tree of Life is holographic, however. There is a complete Tree within every part of you. This means that when you focus on one sphere and tune or heal it, it is healed in every part of your body and soul that is ready to receive it. The qualities each sphere represents are potential within every part of you.

A Brief Overview of the Tree of Life

Follow the Path of the Lightning Bolt on the Qabalah diagram and study the images on it as you read through this chapter. It will help you to gain a first level of understanding. As you continue to read and work with the Qabalah, you will build layers of understanding and experience that will become your own unique perception of the Tree of Life.

Each sphere in your personal Qabalah is a globe of pure being, possessing its own unique qualities and energies. Bigger than a basketball, perhaps the size of a small beach ball, each sphere encompasses a general area on your body and in your aura. Each is the focus for a particular set of soul qualities and potentials that you are in the process of evolving and mastering within your life and over your many incarnations.

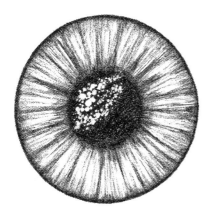

Sphere 1. Kether – Above the crown of your head – the One, Source of Life, God. Here is where the One exists in wholeness. It is also where that One decides to become many individuals and initiates the evolution of life. Kether holds in concept and idea all that will occur through evolution, initiating all things; it also encompasses

the beginning and end of all creation. *Image: The Eye of The One and All of Creation within It*

Sphere 2. Chokmah – To the right side of your head – the Father God. Here is where the angels sing creation into being. Here is created the first individual identity, which I call the Cosmic Christ (a seed within all creation, not particular to any religion), who absolutely knows its unity with the One. It is the seed fertilizing all life, stimulating all of creation through pure spirit, freedom, unconditional love, and wisdom—and present within each individual and each facet of being. *Image: An Angel Singing Creation into Being*

Sphere 3. Binah – To the left side of your head – the Mother God. The Cosmic Womb, Binah births individual beings and life forms out of unity with the One. She births us into the experience of restriction, focus, separation, and individuation. *Image: Looking Through the Doorway of The Cosmic Womb Before Incarnating*

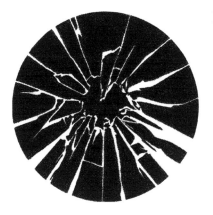

Daat (not a sphere) – In the back of your throat. Daat is a tear in the fabric of reality caused by the fear and isolation we felt when we exited the womb of Binah and entered creation as individual beings. This created feelings of vulnerability and separation from God. *Image: Separation from God – A Fracture in Our Collective Soul*

Sphere 4. Chesed – In your right shoulder area – security, love, vision. This is where we enter into our incarnation and experience security— or the lack of it. This sphere encompasses the influences of family, community, relationships, money, government, education, religion, and fitting into society. Here we learn, or do not learn, to love ourselves and others and to receive love. This is where we receive a vision of our destiny. *Image: Family, Society and Security or the Lack of It*

Sphere 5. Geburah – In your left shoulder area – the force of change. This is where there is an awakening of independent will, personal inner direction, power, and anger as a motivator for change. *Image: Following the Independent Inner Voice to Our Destiny*

Sphere 6. Tipheret – In the middle of your chest and upper abdomen – heart chakra and solar plexus chakra. A focus of self-mastery and the seed of personal Christ consciousness, this sphere integrates and balances the opposite forces within your life, including Higher Self and ego, relationships and independence, mind and emotions. This sphere supports integrity, unity, and Inner Wisdom. *Image: Living From True Center – Unifying Higher Self, Ego, and Opposite Forces Within*

Sphere 7. Netzach – In your right hip area – force of nature. The focus of your instincts, emotions, passions, creative inspirations and impulses, and sexuality, Netzach is also the seat of the creative force of nature

within you. This sphere is often chaotic until integrated with your Inner Wisdom and balanced with your other Qabalah spheres. *Image: The Force of Nature*

Sphere 8. Hod – In your left hip area – left brain, mental focus. This sphere encompasses the ability to focus the energy of your life in a particular direction and follow through and achieve goals. Hod needs to integrate with your Inner Wisdom, intuition, and the rest of your tree so that it works for the greater good and not only its own inclinations. *Image: Bringing Life to Focus – The Camera Lens of the Mind*

Sphere 9. Yesod – In your reproductive area – unconscious seeds of your reality. In this sphere are your heredity, DNA, contracts, beliefs, assumptions, and vows—the elements that define what you will experience in life. *Image: The Seed of Our Experience*

Sphere 10. Malkuth – Below your feet – Earth, physical world. Malkuth receives the seeds that will become our experience from Yesod and grows them within this world. The Earth is a mirror of our beliefs and assumptions about life. To change our experience, we fulfill our contracts and/or update to new contracts as we ascend.

Image: The Earth Grows the Seed We Plant Creating Our Experience

The above provides the briefest understanding of your personal Tree of Life. As you read through the following chapters, which provide more detailed information on the spheres, let your heart and mind begin to integrate a feeling for the spheres as well as a deeper understanding of them. Read, meditate, and read again to build a relationship with the aspect of yourself represented by each sphere on your Qabalah. The Qabalah ascension meditations in the chapter "Tools to Streamline Ascension" will introduce you to the spheres' Archangels, who will help you to heal and ascend into increasing unity with your own Essence of Truth on all levels.

The Healing Qabalah

In this chapter we will journey together through your Tree of Life, getting to know each sphere in more depth and paving the way for some healing and ascension work if you choose. Through the mirror of the Qabalah, you will gain insight into the areas of your soul that require healing and growth. You will see how the opposites on your Tree of Life have been pulling you in different directions and how you can learn to balance and integrate all the forces and powers of your Tree by aligning them with your individual facet of God within.

Sphere 1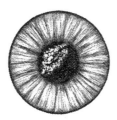

Spirit Home

Kether – Above the Head – The One Source

Deep in your soul, you know the Source, God, is who you are, and is all there is and ever will be. All life is one whole. Kether is that place of oneness that exists at the core of all of life and from which all life springs.

The longing for that oneness, like a desire deep in the core of you to go "home" even though you don't know where or even what home is, is an impulse typical of God within. That God force pulls you back toward oneness with the Source, while driving you forward in your individual evolution through the experience of many lifetimes.

Through the journey of ascension, your body, soul, and spirit will all reunite with God. But long before you return to absolute Oneness in the cosmic sense, you awaken to home within your*self.* God wakes up within you, and you become one with everything while remaining, more than ever, wholly your individual self. This is mastery, and within our bodies and in our lifetimes many of us will experience it as a result of the process of ascension. Others will leave their bodies to begin again with a cleaner and easier agenda in another lifetime. Either way, we are close to achieving a state of mastery within our human experience.

The sphere of Kether on our Tree of Life is the presence of the state of Oneness that exists at the core of all life and from which all life has come.

When we were all One, we decided to become many, to build soul bodies that would be able to hold our many facets within individual selves, to explore life in endless interesting forms. Everything that has happened until now has been the journey of creating soul bodies, capable of knowing unity with God and all other souls and life forms, while sustaining uniqueness and diversity. The ascension process is the fulfillment of that intention. Through these steps, we will heal the wounds caused by the long creative process through many lifetimes and worlds. The construction of souls and worlds is messy; ascension heals the mess and restores sanity and meaning to life.

Kether, the Source, God, exists within the tiniest particles of creation and the largest bodies of life. When the soul of any part of creation is ready to ascend, a seed of God consciousness wakes up within it and begins driving that aspect of life toward the experience of unity with God within itself. In awakening to God within, we awaken to God everywhere within creation, and begin to feel at home in our own bodies and within the world.

The Archangel for the sphere of Kether is Archangel Metatron.

When from the deeps of soul
The spirit turns itself toward being of worlds,
And beauty wells from space-expanses,
Then draws from farthest heavens
The force of life to human bodies,
And joins with mighty action
The spirit's being into human being

– Rudolf Steiner, *Calendar of the Soul*

Sphere 2

Unconditional Love

Chokmah – Right Side of Head – Remember

Chokmah is often called the Father God, although this sphere exists within people of both sexes. It is the activating seed of creation, a force of unconditional love, unity, wisdom, and freedom. It is the place in evolution where God began to manifest into multiple beings. These early beings were pure spirit and lived within a state of unity with God.

I remember being an angel among many other angels, and singing planets into existence. Perhaps this strikes a chord in your memory, too. Our souls began as stars and angels in the long-ago foundations of our universe in the sphere called Chokmah. We were as hands of God, and it was through our agreement and love for God that creation was built. The energy of life in Chokmah is the Holy Spirit, and it is the raw material that generates life. I perceive it as slightly sweet and silvery white, but I feel all the colors of life potential within it. It is as though it were made of fine sugar crystals shining gently and refracting colors, like snow in sunlight on a slightly misty morning. The Holy Spirit is rich with potential and ready to burst into life at the right opportunity.

Memory – A Chokmah Experience

Dusk. I am lying on the floor in the midst of a personal Healing Qabalah meditation. My soul has briefly left my body, and as I return to awareness of it, I find myself floating in a sea of gently rolling waves of crystalline energy.

Silvery and pearlescent, the waves seem to hold all colors within them. The energy stimulates my skin, my aura, and my very soul. I am filled with awe. "What is this?" I ask, and it comes to me that this is what Patricia Waldygo drew within Chokmah in her poster, "The Kabbalistic Tree of Life." *It is the most wholesome and enlivening energy I have ever felt, and all I can do is smile and float within the joy of it.*

The energy I encountered in this meditation is the Holy Spirit, and it is the substance out of which form is built. Its opalescent and crystalline qualities remind me of the process of making rock candy, when the water becomes so saturated with sugar that it is almost ready to form into candy crystals. This substance is all potential and absolute love; it is wholesome, clean, and filled with joy. At certain points in the ascension process, this energy appears just after the old energies have cleared and when there is a void that is ready to be filled with the new world energy. When that point is reached, the Holy Spirit flows into those places and initiates the creation of the new world within it.

The Cosmic Christ,* a foundational level of divine individuality and unity present within all life, is the first independent being who was conceived out of the One within Kether and birthed within Chokmah. The seed that carries God consciousness and true intent into all of creation, the Cosmic Christ, is present at the core of all life. It knows its oneness with God as well as its own individual identity. The Christ consciousness within each soul is the seed that awakens us to our ascension and reunification with God within our individual selves. The Holy Spirit is the substance through which the Cosmic Christ moves into creation and through which it can act.

As we ascend to unity with the True Source of Life, while still within our human experience, we once again become cocreators with God in a way similar to when we were angels. But where angels are like individual hands directed by the One Source without independent will, ascension will allow us to join with God as independent souls working from within the creation. God will eventually awaken as independent identities through each life form, and life will begin to fulfill its true potential in earnest.

*The Cosmic Christ is not dependent on any religious orientation; you may use a different name to represent this truth.

Two Visions and a Miracle

Vision

I am sitting in my favorite chair, and suddenly the one who is unmistakably Jesus has a hand on each of the chair arms and is looking into my eyes. The body language is imposing, but the energy is respectful, kind, and open, with a hint of a humorous smile at the corners of his mouth.

Having been brought up by a psychologically imbalanced, raging, Pentecostal Missionary mother, I gave up on not only the religion but also *anything related to it. However, I have always known Jesus in the core of my being and that he was not like the elements of religion I didn't agree with.*

Even so, I asked him to please go away; I wasn't quite ready to deal with him yet. So he left and left me with a slightly humorous smile curling at the corners of my mouth.

Vision

I am taking a shower at my mothers' house a few days after the earlier vision (and I mean no disrespect by what I am going to tell you; this is what actually happened!). Suddenly Jesus is in the shower with me. Long wavy dark hair, olive skin typical of his people, and I didn't dare look to see if he had on his loin cloth—I didn't want to know.

I laugh and say, "I guess you are trying to tell me you are nothing like my mother said you are!"

Now I am comfortable with him, but I still don't use his name a lot, because religion insists that you must, and so I simply can't. I will not be pushed around by people's religious threats! And I have observed that people use the name and yet having their own agendas. Or, not knowing the truth, they may connect with something else entirely. I know the energy of the Christ and call it forth by its clean, true, and unconditionally loving presence within all life where God has planted it for us to find by whatever name we call it.

Miracle

Later that same week driving in heavy traffic, I find myself caught in an impossible situation where it seems clear that I can't avoid having my car crushed by an oncoming van.

Just as I'm saying goodbye to life, I find myself a block away, safely driving down the road.

It is suddenly clear to me that this is why Jesus needed to make a connection with me this week in particular. He has just picked my car up and moved it a block, and I suppose I must have to be open to him for that to happen! (I had heard of a similar miracle happening to some friends of mine on a mountain pass in Colorado.) Now I know that I am safely here in this body until the time comes for me to leave, and I guess that time hasn't come yet. What a relief!

While I am an ordained minister, I don't ever put God or Christ in a religious box. I also know that by whatever name we call it, the Christ is within all of us. I know that we are all eternal and beloved by the Creator, of whom we are each intimately a part for all eternity and beyond. Achieving Christ Consciousness, which is the state of unity with the One while being absolutely and uniquely oneself, has been accomplished by many souls and will ultimately be experienced by every soul, somewhere along their evolution through lifetimes. This is the ultimate goal of ascension and happens regardless of religious affiliations or the term you use for this enlightened state.

Within the universe, there are billions of beings who are called Christ. As a title, it recognizes a level of evolution in which a soul has reunited with God within its individual self. There are many names for those who have achieved this level of soul. Master, Ascended Master, or Buddha are some that I perceive as accurate. There is also the Cosmic Christ, father of all souls in Chokmah.

Vision 1 from Chokmah: Looking into Binah

We are angels in Chokmah at the very beginning of creation. We have loved being expressions of God's perfect love and intention, and it has been all of our desire and our only experience. Having always known ourselves as extensions of the One Source of Life's own intentions, we are slightly shocked when that One plants within our hearts what feels like a subversive idea to create something of our own design, something that has not been thought of by God.

As this idea emerges within us (created by God, but that is not how we feel it), we see in our inner vision the sphere of Binah emerging as a great and powerful unknown, the birthplace of something absolutely new.

This is the beginning of the journey of separation and of incarnation into individual forms possessing independent self-will. Through many lifetimes and many worlds, this journey will ultimately lead to the experience that we know now as ascension, the journey of reuniting with the Source of All Life manifest within many individual life forms. The vision above is a memory from the beginning of creation. It is of God's initiation of independent thought, creating independent soul vehicles, so the One could begin to self-actualize within many life forms.

Now through ascension, in order to reunite with the wholeness of life, we have to overcome a sense of shame and guilt. There is a primal belief that our experience of separation from unity with God is a punishment for acting under what we thought was our own will to create something different from God, the One. Recognizing in retrospect that we were and are innocent—since it is God within us who planted the seed of independent will and separation—we can forgive ourselves. We can learn to accept forgiveness from God for all actions and events that have brought pain and separation throughout all our lifetimes. Through this forgiveness we reunite with God, the One, and through that with all of creation, and all pain and loneliness is healed.

Our self-will is an aspect of the will of the One, developing within us our potential to be cocreators through the journey of separation. Then, through the ascension process, our self-will matures into a more perfect expression of the Essence of Truth that is God, expressing—uniquely within each individual life and collectively within the world—an experience of harmony and unity and Oneness right here on Earth.

Vision 2 from Chokmah: The Creation of Conflict and Opposition

There was another group of angels within Chokmah who were also called into individual incarnations. Instead of independent self-will, they were given a seed of judgment for those who had it. They were called into the experience of life to be an oppositional force, controlling and restricting the independent and creative impulses of the independent group.

As they entered into the created world and individual incarnations, they came with a judgment that the creation was wrong. They blamed the other group for causing separation from God, but they also felt jealous of what they saw as the more creative and independent role the others had. They felt they had a duty to control and squelch the natural impulses within people and the world in general.

This group initiated social structures, religious controls and judgments, governments, finances, and other systems that limited and focused the more expansive energies of the independent group.

Both groups were needed; both were initiated by the One. Both feel oppressed and judgmental toward the other, and they blame each other for the discomfort that they feel is caused by behaviors in the other that *they think are wrong.*

Here we find the initiation of war and strife. These two groups of competing forces sometimes seem like pinballs in the great pinball machine of life, bouncing off of each other and forcing each to grow in necessary ways. My gentle father's favorite Bible quote comes to mind: "In pressure hast thou enlarged me" (Psalm 4:1).

The pressures of these conflicts have been essential in directing us toward our necessary soul development goals. Once we forgot our unity with the One and began acting upon our own limited perspectives, we required the oppositional force to keep us moving in the directions we needed to go and to keep us from permanently being lost within the created experience and separate from God indefinitely. Once we awaken to the unique facet of God within us and begin to be directed from a place of Inner Wisdom and truth, the pinball machine of opposition within our lives becomes unnecessary and can gradually be released from our experience.

Over time, our souls have taken on qualities of both groups. Now we need to integrate and balance these forces, allowing the unique facet of God within each one of us to achieve mastery of our power and independent will and fulfill our true destiny of wholeness.

Vision 2 from Chokmah – Part B: The Forces of Creation and Death and Their Resolution in the New World

Another facet of the oppositional lines of incarnation born within Chokmah could be expressed by calling these two forces Creation and Death.

The creative line invests divine energy into the creation of life forms, but in the old world state of separation and forgetfulness, it often becomes identified with that creation and forgets about its spiritual nature as a part of God.

To prevent the incarnate aspects of God from losing themselves indefinitely within the creation, the oppositional force generated the experience of death, to free our spirits to return to Oneness.

As we ascend, every aspect of life awakens gradually to a state of unity with the Source of Life in Oneness, while retaining its unique identity and independent function as an individual life form. Eventually, the need for the oppositional force and the processes of death become unnecessary. In the new world state, souls will ascend their individual forms and return to Oneness at will, whenever they are ready. There will be no more forgetfulness of who we really are; every aspect of life will be clear on that count, down to the smallest particle of life. So the experiences of disease, war, suffering, and death will become obsolete and gradually be worked out of our bodies and our world.

The Archangel for the sphere of Chokmah is Archangel Ratziel

Sphere 3

Forgetting

Binah – Left Side of Head – Cosmic Womb

Imagine you are standing at a natural stone arch (one like Delicate Arch in Arches National Park in Utah). It is a clear night, and through the arch you see a black velvet sky pierced by points of colored light from the stars. You can feel your energy focused and being drawn through the arch as you enter a universe set with possibilities and experiences you can't yet imagine or foresee. There is a feeling of inevitability. You trust, and yet are nervous, knowing you will be challenged over and over again so that you may realize your potential.

This is probably not so far removed from our actual experience transiting through the sphere of Binah, the cosmic womb, on our way to the incarnations we are living now. She is the Mother God and the medium of transition from unity into individuality. As with any birth, fear and pain are usually involved. Coming out of Binah, we find ourselves alone for the first time. This is our soul's first trauma, and the memory of it is deep within each of us. That memory initiates a compulsion within us to seek a place where we feel whole and safe. That compulsion will ultimately motivate us to find God within and pull us toward the destiny we have planned for our lives.

As we transition along the Path of the Lightning Bolt out of Chokmah and through Binah, we begin the journey into our individual lifetimes. Our consciousness of self is focused toward the body we will enter in Chesed. Our intentions are set, and our contracts are entered into for the development of the particular soul qualities and strengths we will need to become the vehicle God desires us to be, once we reach the point of ascension and reunification.

Having entered a physical body, as we look out at life through the limited senses and consciousness it possesses, we forget that we are the creators of this experience; we tend to feel more the victims of it. But through this experience within many lifetimes and worlds, our souls evolve and begin to ascend. At the point where God begins to wake up within our bodies and souls, we are increasingly able to rediscover unity with God; only now we know it within our bodies and the world in which we live!

Healing the wounds of separation that originated in Binah is a journey we must travel to return to unity with the All That Is. Ascension initiates a process of forgiveness and healing for all the pain and fear we have experienced on our many journeys of life.

The experience we have with our human mothers is a microcosm of our relationship with the cosmic mother Binah. It holds many opportunities that bring to focus the beliefs and hurts from our past, to help us learn to heal and forgive those primal wounds of separation. You can use the Qabalah ascension meditations in the chapter "Tools to Streamline Ascension" to begin to heal and ascend your Binah and all your Qabalah spheres, if you are so inclined.

Within our lives, each time we leave behind the comfort and security of the familiar to venture into the unknown, we experience yet again the opportunity, which began in Binah, to overcome fear and separation and find confidence in the wisdom, strength, and benevolence of God within. This leads us on to the next stage of our growth.

The Archangel for the sphere of Binah is Archangel Tzaphkiel

A Fracture

Fear

Daat – Back of Throat – God has left us here alone

Exiting the womb of Binah, we leave our natural state of pure spirit and suddenly feel cut off from God and that sense of unity with everything that is. In Binah we felt an initial separation, almost like falling asleep into a deep dream. In Daat, we experience the separation as a shock, an awakening to a totally new state that makes us feel terrifyingly alone. Daat is the transition between spirit and form, during which we are in danger of panicking and losing ourselves in the fear or anger that God has abandoned or rejected us.

As stated above, God hasn't really rejected us; we are God, seeking to differentiate into many individuals. The belief in separation is a transitional tool to achieve this end. It forces individuals to learn to function independently and to build the soul bodies that will allow God to wake up within many individuals on many worlds.

Daat is like a fracture in our souls that creates a chasm between our individual lives and the unity we crave. This is where our darkest experiences of life originate and are born out of our fear, hopelessness, and despair. Here we find the roots of destructive behaviors, such as violence, abuse, addiction, and the misuse of sex, power, and our spiritual gifts. These experiences cement our false belief in separation and force those aspects of our souls that have resisted the notion of separation to let go of the previously known unity with God in pure spirit, so that we may one day find a new unity with God here within our incarnate experience.

The journey of ascension allows us to transition back through Daat to heal these wounds. When the ascension timer goes off and our own unique facet of God begins to awaken within our souls, we find within us a growing trust and faith in our own truth and the eternal love of the One Source. We begin to let go of our darkest fears of unworthiness, anger at God for the suffering in life, and judgment of ourselves and others. The healing of these things is the healing of Daat within us, and we begin to know unity with Our Source in all aspects of our lives again.

The Archangel for the Daat is Archangel Liestrom

Sphere 4

Security, Family, Society, Relationships

Chesed– Right Shoulder– Incarnating

Having passed through the womb of Binah and the fear of Daat, we enter the sphere of Chesed, where we are born into a body, a family, and a society. Here we find security or we don't; love, or the lack of it; provision or scarcity; and our relationships. Our experiences are defined by the contracts our personal facet of God has made. The intentions of these soul contracts are to develop soul muscles and qualities that will ultimately enable our personal facet of the One to awaken and self-actualize within our individual soul bodies. For example, if a soul needs to learn how to be a leader and strongly independent, some of its incarnations will include great challenges to overcome, to give it the opportunity to develop the needed soul qualities and muscles.

The lessons of Chesed are often to get along, go along, conform, please others, do what we are told, and make a place for ourselves within the society, community, and family through religion, education, finances, and so forth. Our goals at this basic level are generally to feel secure and to experience love and approval. When we experience those things, we learn to feel good about ourselves, but we may become dependent and too attached to the comfort and security of conformity. When we don't experience them, we become more independent and have to access greater inner strength. Ultimately, we need to balance both extremes in order to be our empowered selves and to be loved, too.

Within the conformity of Chesed is a seed of independent vision that shows us a destiny beyond where we are but doesn't tell us how to get there. It draws us toward the next step in our evolution, which is Geburah, where we discover our own inner direction. Our consciousness in Chesed may be inclined to wait for someone to tell us what to do or expect a secure transition from the present into our future. But taking the step toward our destiny requires us to follow that independent vision, which directs us through a transition like Daat (only not as extreme). We have to let go of security and follow our independent inner wisdom.

The Archangel for the sphere of Chesed is Archangel Tzadkiel

Sphere 5

Geburah – Left Shoulder – Breaking Through

Somewhere between the ages of ten and sixty-five, we realize that there is something unique within our souls that can't be fulfilled by merely fitting in and doing what seems to be right by the standards of family, society, religion, or our work places. The hole that has existed deep within us since our transition through Binah and Daat continues to nag us. It can't be filled from without but requires us to go within and follow our deeper impulses toward wholeness. When that happens, Geburah wakes up to help us learn to say *no* to all the good things we "should be doing" and all the distractions that we want but that aren't really good for us and *yes* to the things within our soul that we must do in order to grow and be true to ourselves.

Within Geburah is the part of our souls that some call *the still, small voice*. It knows what steps to take in each moment to reach the visions of our destinies that we perceived in Chesed. It calls us forward against all odds and often contrary to the desires of family and community. It leads us inevitably toward a realization of our own truth and potential. It breaks the chains of habit, conformity, and obligation and moves us toward our destinies.

Any time we need the strength to move ahead, or we know we need to make a change but aren't sure in which direction to go, the answers lie within us. If we invest our hearts and minds in listening and following the deep inner will that we own through Geburah, we will find the answers we need. Geburah requires us to trust ourselves and take one step at a time in the direction we sense is right. During this process, we may lose sight of the independent vision we had in Chesed, but the direction we should follow lies in the subtleties of our hearts and our bellies (belly feelings are powerful and clear; listen to them!) and our will.

If we don't listen and follow the direction we feel within, the powerful force of change inherent within Geburah will eventually turn against us. We may become angry or bitter or have health challenges. Our souls won't let us avoid the responsibility of following our inner direction. The sooner we learn to listen and follow our souls' direction, the smoother our journeys will be! Geburah calls us toward our cores and our truths.

Our inner direction supersedes our mental concepts of what we want to do. It is a deep, accurate, and true sense of purpose. Watch out for ideals we hold that are based on what we have seen others do; they may be helpful or not. We are unique, and within us is something only we can be. If it appears to be like someone else, that appearance will only be surface; underneath it your truth will be fresh and uniquely yours. You will know what it is through the finely tuned guide within, which is your Geburah, a place of feeling, power, and an inner drive toward truth. Practice using Geburah in all your little choices, so that when it comes to the big ones you will have the muscle well developed and can follow it accurately.

Allegory

The View from the Mountaintop and the Pilgrimage of Self-Actualization

The sphere of Chesed on our Tree of Life is the place where we grow up, where we learn to fit into society and make a place for ourselves in the world with greater or lesser success. As our evolution through Chesed begins to motivate us toward Geburah, which calls us to our souls' individuation, we may feel an impulse toward something new, or **have a vision as from a mountain top**, where we see beyond all we have known to an experience we feel destined to know. That vision holds for us all of our longing, and the sense that fulfillment is possible beyond the restrictions of our daily lives.

For the purpose of our story, we will use a metaphor of the ocean for our destiny. Our vision from the mountaintop tells us our destiny is to experience the ocean. So we leave the place of our birth and walk down from the metaphorical mountaintop of our vision, desiring to fulfill our destiny—and there we encounter a forest at the foot of the mountain. This is a metaphor for **our first obstruction**. We didn't expect the forest; we thought we were going to the ocean. That is enough to send a lot of people back up the mountain with an attitude that they just can't trust their inner vision and they are better off staying within the bounds of their familiar lives. For others, this is the place where they adjust their priorities, hone their sense of purpose, and continue on through the confusing and intimidating forest.

Geburah is the aspect of our soul that knows how to move toward our soul's purpose and destiny, even when we've lost the vision of our goal in the forest of life's experiences. It is that still small voice that tells us how to navigate through the unknown and the dangerous: put your foot here, then step there, don't let the wolf smell your fear, and so on.

If we listen to Geburah within, we will continue on through the forest and eventually hit the thicket, **the second obstruction**. A thicket is a painful thing to go through, causing scratches and making us very uncomfortable. This obstacle may be enough to send many people back home, never to leave again.

If we make it through the thicket, however, we will encounter **the third obstruction**: an unpleasant, wet, and stinking swamp. By this time, it may be too difficult to turn back, and some of us will continue on out of sheer stubbornness, desperation, or faith. Others will give up and become stuck or resort to drink and drugs. For those who continue, there is a deepening commitment and faith that can grow while crossing the swamp, although it can be a time of great hardship, disappointment, or loneliness. These hardships make souls strong and resilient—if they don't allow themselves to grow bitter and resentful instead.

With great perseverance, we near the far side of the swamp, and we hear a new sound—the sound of waves hitting the beach. This new sound calls us to our destiny and rewards us with warm sand and sunlight on waves, the ocean.

For the souls who have followed their calling and endured its challenges, Geburah leads us to a place of increased strength and personal authority. Denying the call brings

sadness, dissatisfaction, and grief. Following that call may be very difficult, but the rewards are great. The journey through these challenges prepares you to enter the next phase of your evolution in the sphere of Tipheret.

We all journey through these stages many times to develop deeper levels of self-awareness and personal authority.

The Archangel for the sphere of Geburah is Archangel Khamael

Sphere 6

The Potential for Mastery

Tipheret – Center Torso – Unity, God Within

Imagine the solar system without the sun—true chaos. That would be our Tree of Life without Tipheret. The magnetism of the sun, due to its great size, weight, and energy, holds the planets of our solar system in their orbits, so that they don't fly away or collide with each other.

As the sun is the true center of our solar system, so Tipheret is the true center of our Tree of Life. And like the sun, Tipheret's job is to hold the Tree of Life's other spheres and their various powers in their right relationships within our lives. These spheres represent the many forces that pull us from within. Through Tipheret, we can come to master these often opposing forces and get everything pulling in the right direction.

In Chesed, our energy is centered on what is necessary to sustain self, family, and community. Geburah takes us beyond that focus, seeking something more. The something more we are seeking may be realized within Tipheret.

Tipheret is where we find our individual facets of God. Through identifying with Tipheret and living from that inner truth, we can find mastery within our lives. That mastery is already present as a personal seed of the Cosmic Christ that you own from your beginnings in Chokmah. So, achieving mastery is a combination of pure awakening and personal diligence. There are two aspects of Tipheret, and both are important. The first, which is related to the heart chakra, is the presence of our Inner Wisdom or our personal focus of Christ (this individuated God consciousness has many names). Here is the place where we simply know what is true. It is our inner compass that always points toward true north. There is no element more essential to our spiritual development and the fulfillment of our purpose in life than this part of us. Through this aspect of Tipheret, we can access and integrate into our lives all wisdom, insight, and information needed about anything and everything in the universe, because it is connected to All That Is. This is also the center of healing; through this inner connection with God, we can release our suffering and reconnect to our true eternal unity and wholeness, which brings healing on all levels.

The second aspect, which is related to the solar plexus chakra, is that sense of ourselves in the world as individual identities or what is commonly called ego. A strong sense of self is an essential foundation on which to grow spiritually. Ego gets a bad rap in many spiritual faiths, because it can trap people within their material experiences. However, without a healthy ego, a soul awakening to its oneness with All That Is can expand until the soul gets lost within the psychic energies of the world. The soul may get too spacey or sensitive and absorb other people's feelings and energy. Then they can be easily manipulated and energetically drained by those with strong psychic energy. Or, in the worst-case scenario, the loss of self-definition can lead to a psychotic break. We can't be spiritually strong in the world without a reasonably healthy ego. For those desiring to grow spiritually and ascend into unity with God and all of life, a clear sense of who *I am* is an essential anchor for maintaining the integrity of their individual selves.

Within Tipheret, these two essential focuses of who *I am* need to learn to work together:

> **Heart Chakra:** *I am an unlimited spiritual being centered on eternal truth and connected with all of life;*
>
> and
>
> **Solar Plexus Chakra:** *I am a distinct individual person living in a physical body. I am responsible for maintaining myself in all ways, including my physical, mental, emotional, and spiritual health, and for establishing healthy boundaries in relationship to others.*

As these two elements of Tipheret mature and partner together within our lives and souls, our Tipheret gains the weight, substance, and energy to more ably hold the spheres on the Tree of Life in their proper orbits, like the sun holds the planets in theirs. With effort and commitment to maintaining this union of divine and human identity, our souls gain balance and unity within all aspects of ourselves. Their unique focus of God within can then be invited to direct our lives. This is the foundation of spiritual mastery.

Love for and commitment to ourselves and our lives are essential, not in a narcissistic way but in a balanced and responsible way. For many, holding onto ourselves and being true to ourselves are much harder than losing ourselves in service to others. Service to others will be more impactful when it comes from a balanced unity with God within rather than from a state of self-abandonment. Healing our sense of self-worth, whether it is too great or too little, is an important ingredient of the ascension process. In some ways it will happen naturally as we grow, and in some ways we may have to do some deep soul searching—reconnecting with God and love and releasing old wounds and shame.

The journey of ascension will ultimately bring all of us into increased mastery within our bodies and within the world. The long journey of incarnation and all the challenges we have experienced during it have been developing our souls to the point where our own facet of God could awaken within our bodies and lives. When we are ready, we will join with God also awakened within others to recreate the world at a higher and more enjoyable level than the one we have known thus far.

A True Story of Choices

Very early in my career as a healer, a woman with advanced cancer contacted me. I will call her Anna, although that is not her real name, and I have changed elements of the story to protect her identity. Anna had been released from the hospital with morphine; nothing else could be done for her. Using my spiritual vision, I described her cancer to her. She confirmed that what I saw was consistent with what her X-rays had revealed.

Working on Anna was unusual in that she put out no personal energy. It was almost like working on a mirror; the only energy I felt was the energy I put out myself. But one day during her healing, a fountain of beautiful golden energy sprang out of her solar plexus! When I asked her what had changed, she said she had decided to leave her relationship. It was obvious that this was a good idea and that she was coming back to life.

Following that change, Anna recovered so quickly and fully that there was no longer any indication on her X-rays that the cancer had ever existed.

A few years later, I called Anna to tell her that I was now teaching spiritual healing in addition to performing my healing work. She informed me that she had returned to her relationship and now had a new form of cancer. When I reminded her that she had been through this before and asked what she planned to do, she hung up on me.

I never spoke with Anna again. I don't know what happened to her, but if she didn't change her course of action, I can guess the outcome. What happened in the short run was pretty obvious and illustrates an important element of the transition through Chesed, Geburah, and Tipheret on the Tree of Life.

Let's consider Anna's story relative to the Tree of Life, using the allegory of the view from the mountaintop and the journey of self-actualization. We can look at the choices she made and the lessons it holds for many of us.

We will begin in the sphere of Chesed. Anna's husband was a political leader. He was also a pathological liar, according to Anna. As his wife and a member of their political party, Anna was required to be obedient, respectful, pleasing, and all the things required of a good wife and mother. In order to maintain the status quo of a wealthy and successful political family, Anna repressed her despair at ever getting what she personally needed on the deeper levels. When her children grew up and moved away, the emptiness and hopelessness she felt blossomed into cancer.

Cancer is frequently an expression of the belief that *It is easier for me to die than to get what I need out of life*. This belief may be conscious, unconscious, or something carried through heredity and the soul group. But wherever it manifests that belief is what allows the cancer to grow.

At a certain point, Anna's Geburah kicked in and her soul chose life over her marriage, and she journeyed through the metaphorical forest, the thicket, and the swamp to her personal experience of the ocean. Through that journey, she reclaimed her power to live and recovered fully from cancer.

However, once at the place of her destiny—which is the next sphere, Tipheret—she failed to thrive. She was now the leader in her own life, and rather than grasping that destiny and continuing to grow her soul, she longed for the familiar habits of her past. The seduction of habits and their familiarity is great, and it can be difficult to realize that we need to keep growing once we reach adulthood. In fact, to stop growing is to begin dying, and that is what Anna found. We must create new habits and discover the deeper satisfaction that comes from living in our truth and our power throughout our lives. Life is a series of stages through which we work out the lessons of our soul development. We must keep following the inner voice of Geburah wherever it takes us and enjoy the journey that keeps us vibrant and alive each day of our lives. If we stop growing, our lives may become deadly dull and depressing. Through this process you will grow new soul muscles and capacities your Higher Self needs, as you ascend into your true potential.

We don't have to give up the love and security of Chesed to claim ourselves as independently guided and unique in Geburah. There is a place of true center in our Inner Wisdom within

Tipheret. There we can balance the need for security, love, and comfort with the openness to change and awareness of our souls' truth and destiny. In bringing these into balance, we find the wholeness and satisfaction that we miss when we get stuck in one extreme or the other.

The journey of balance is a moment-by-moment awareness by which we stay honest and responsible in the choices we make for ourselves. We must always inquire within our hearts and bellies about what the correct responses are to the choices and circumstances in our lives. In this way, we learn to say yes to the right things and to lovingly and firmly say no to those things that distract us from our truths.

~~~~~~~~~~~~~~~~~~~

As we continue on our journey down the Tree of Life, below the lower half of Tipheret (the solar plexus chakra), we enter our lower consciousness. Following the Path of the Lightning Bolt, which takes us further and further from the experience of unity with God, we enter our animal self. Our physical body, instincts, and mind are the consciousness of our material life on earth.

It is trickier to awaken God consciousness within these aspects of ourselves than it is from the top of Tipheret (the heart chakra) and the higher spheres on our tree. This is because the lower energies are so driven by the forces of nature and instinct that they have difficulty noticing anything that doesn't reach them at those levels. Generally, these lower parts of us are programmed genetically to respond to the needs of our physical bodies and insure that physical life continues on Earth.

Integrating these lower aspects of self with our higher consciousness is essential for God to be able to create within the world, so awakening at this level has been a prime directive on Earth over the past 150 years or so. During this time, psychology, homeopathy, the use of flower essences, and spiritualism have burgeoned, along with the gradual awakening of intuition and of spirituality beyond religion. We have also experienced the sexual revolution and the breaking down of gender roles. These changes have allowed women, who tend to be more awake at these levels, to increasingly influence our society. Similarly, they have contributed to a softening of male roles and a greater awakening to feeling and intuition for men. All of these developments have helped us evolve beyond the duality of pure animal instinct and its opposite, the tendency to repress instinct and live in our heads. They have helped us begin to integrate higher consciousness into our unconscious and lower levels of self.

As we awaken to our truth on these lower levels of vibration, we gain not only great spiritual and social influence but also access to many aspects of our healing and growth that were only partially resolved when working exclusively in the higher vibrations. Integrating these lower levels will help us become whole, strong, balanced, and capable of fulfilling our true vision and purpose in the world.

The Archangel for the sphere of Tipheret is Archangel Michael

Sphere 7

Chaos/Creativity

Netzach – Right Hip – The Force of Nature

The Netzach Experience, Part 1

As we begin to wake up in Netzach, we immediately become aware of a greater feeling of aliveness. Like the feeling we get when we have spent a long time within nature; there is a deeper sense of grounded relaxation, power, and awareness of life in our bodies and within the world. The energy in Netzach is constantly changing, like the weather. It has waves of emotion, sensation, passion, inspiration, and willpower alternating with a deep lethargy and inclination to stop thinking and striving. It can be compelling just to be immersed within all the sensations of life within the physical world, or alternately to withdraw and hide from it all.

Netzach is chaos and creativity. She is emotion, feeling, instinct, and sexuality, the force of nature within us. Finding mastery within Netzach is a bit like building a safe and cooperative relationship with a wild horse. Netzach is infinitely powerful and can be our best friend. She can also be destructive if we don't carefully tend our relationship with this essential part of our nature.

Because Netzach is so powerful and chaotic, there is an inclination to suppress this aspect of our life force. We may be inclined to live in a strictly rational space in our minds that denies the wisdom within our instincts and emotions. Or we may prefer to live in our higher chakra centers to maintain the clarity that comes from a high vibration that more easily stays in touch with the spiritual world. Both of these behaviors help us avoid the potential downfalls present within this aspect of ourselves. Where we have been psychologically and instinctually damaged, we may choose to dissociate from memories and feelings that reside at this level of our bodies and souls. However, without Netzach's creative force in our lives, things become dull and stagnant; they begin to die. Netzach is the power that animates life within the world and the innate wisdom that stimulates natural evolution within physical form.

There have always been those who are committed deeply to this aspect of life, which sometimes leads to their own destruction. It is within Netzach that we are stimulated toward artistic and other creative expression. When people have emotional, creative, or artistic inclinations without sufficient physical or spiritual discipline and direction, however, chaos can ensue. The creative power of Netzach can become submerged in the pleasures and pains of the body and senses, often leading to addictive and self-destructive behaviors.

When people have been deeply wounded in Netzach, their power and instincts can become twisted. They may become violent and destructive toward themselves and others.

Because Netzach embodies creation and the preservation of life, we find here the drive to fulfill basic needs. This is the part of us that responds to food, sex, the need for security, and the desire to escape discomfort and danger. It is where our instincts, the power of fight or flight, and competition all reside. It is also where desire can become obsession or addiction. In order to grow, we must balance these essential aspects of life with a higher perspective and purpose through integration with our higher spiritual consciousness.

The Netzach Experience Part 2

Netzach is full of opportunity and risk. There is nothing dull about this aspect of our lives! The best solution I have found to the potential problems of Netzach is to welcome God to bring higher focus, direction, and protection into this very earthy level of our being. When focused in the right way, Netzach brings a sweet richness, variety, beauty, and fullness to life that makes it well worth living.

The power of Netzach within us can become a song of love and passion for the Divine Core present within all life forms. It can be a willingness to live a life that our facet of God would want to share. This is infinitely better than letting all the juice and joy leak out of ourselves, because we are so focused on the dull requirements of living that life becomes like a hard old raisin no one can even chew. In order for our unique facets of God to work through our lives and make them prosperous and worth living, we need to make time to enjoy our lives, to surrender, and trust. I think this old saying makes a very Netzachian point:

Dance as if no one were watching
Sing as if no one were listening
Live every day as if it were your last!

Netzach is a force. It has vast power and creative potential, and life is dull without it. Left to its own devices, however, it is a bit too much energy with not enough direction and follow-through. So as we leave Netzach, which is focused in our right hip, and move across the tree (and our pelvis) to the left hip, we find ourselves coming to focus in the sphere of Hod.

The Archangel for the sphere of Netzach is Archangel Haniel

If the Tree of Life were a camera, Netzach would be the batteries, without which the camera would have no power. Hod would be the focusing lens, without which the picture would be blurry. Tipheret would be the hand that holds the camera and the eye coordinating all the gifts of the artist. The film belongs to your personal facet of God to create something meaningful, beautiful, and life-enhancing.

Sphere 8

The Camera's Lens

Hod – Left Hip – The Mind, Focus, Follow-Through

Hod is the mind, and it needs to find its right place within the wholeness of our being. I spent the first six years of my healing career teaching people to get out of their heads and into their feelings, instincts, and intuition, where they would find a connection to God within and be able to heal. I finally realized I needed to understand what the mind is supposed to do, rather than seeing it as rigid, controlling, and separating us from our feelings and intuition. When I asked God to clarify it for me, I was given the camera lens analogy.

Contrary to what has generally been assumed for centuries in Western culture, the mind was not designed to run the show

in our lives. It is designed to be an interface and a focus of a much more comprehensive system for actualizing the greater good within life. Expecting the mind to originate ideas and manifest everything on its own is a lot like expecting the camera to take a picture with only the focusing lens and no batteries, intelligent eye and hand, or film.

Memory – Osprey

Having just arrived at a favorite park near my home in southeast Michigan, I am ready to walk in the lovely woods around clear and shallow Crooked Lake. It starts to sprinkle, and I return to the car. Opening the door, I look up and see a fish hawk flying over the lake. An unlikely sight in this location and at this time before its recovery in Michigan, the osprey is beautiful. I am instantly alert because an osprey has recently come to me in a vision, and I didn't understand its message. Now is my opportunity to learn. I am ready.

Watching the osprey, I am struck by its power and focus. It circles above the lake, gazing intently at the water, then hovers alert, from a hundred feet up, head down. Suddenly it dives straight into the water and comes up with a fish in its talons! It flies across the lake to feast in a tree.

The hawk's patience, timing, precision, and follow-through are a revelation of the correct function of Hod. The powerful, instinctual osprey (Netzach), with wholeness and balance (Tipheret), has the powerful focus (Hod) to act at exactly the right moment to catch the fish.

When our hearts do not trust in God's presence, wisdom, and love within the world, we will function from our ego. From that perspective there seem to be two choices in life: animal instinct or mental control. Relying on mental control has been less chaotic and therefore seemed the better choice in many cultures. But the results of this approach have been devastating both socially and for the planet. A world in which the emotional, instinctual, and creative elements of life (Netzach) are repressed or controlled by the linear and often rigid elements of the mind (Hod) without spiritual guidance and inspiration is increasingly barren, destructive, and self-defeating. Alternately, a world without the mind (Hod) as focus, and without God within (Tipheret) as director, creates chaos. Our osprey would starve, lacking the patience and focus to catch a fish.

As we begin to wake up to the presence of the divine within our human experience, we can bring both Hod and Netzach—mind/focus and emotion/instinct—into their optimal relationship within ourselves and our world. Creation without both elements guided from a higher perspective just doesn't work very well. But together, the result is a beautiful picture taken by the most powerful and refined camera ever built.

Hod, like the lens of a camera, is the point in our souls where all the powerful influences from every sphere on our Tree of Life come to a point of choice. Looking through the camera lens of our lives, what are we trying to create? What does God within us desire to do? Out of all the creative possibilities and things we love in our passionate, Netzachian selves, and out of all the possibilities our minds can think of, what is the proper focus for our lives in this moment?

In order to answer this question, we have to ask ourselves, "Who is the artist taking this picture?" If it is our emotional self, the answer will be one thing; if it is our mental self, it will be another. Neither one will satisfy both parts of us. If we go to a higher orientation through Tipheret, however, we will find the place within our soul where resides a true and balanced core of our eternal and divine self. There we will be able to get the answer that satisfies us and fulfills our greater purpose.

So Hod, ideally, is a place where all of the higher influences on our tree find agreement; these include Tipheret which understands our life's purpose, the still small voice of Geburah, the inspiration and creative drive within Netzach, and the other higher spheres on our Tree of Life all come to focus and follow-through in Hod. When the mind is open and receptive to these higher influences, it is guided to adjust the lens to create the best picture for our lives.

The Archangel for the sphere of Hod is Archangel Raphael

Sphere 9

The Seed

Yesod– Reproductive Area – Contracts

Deep in the unconscious, Yesod contains the pattern for or seed of our experience of life. This foundation of our experience is defined by heredity, the soul contracts our Higher Self has chosen for our evolution in this and all of our lifetimes, and the assumptions we have acquired in our experiences in present and past lives. As our life force inexorably flows through us to create our lives, it is molded by these inner structures into a seed that will grow within the world of our experience. The Earth, good mother that she is, takes that seed, and in unconditional love births whatever forms we have planted within the substance of her living womb. Then we see our contracts, beliefs, and assumptions mirrored back to us through the experiences of our lives.

Soul Contracts

As a healer, I learned early on to clear energy that was not in harmony within my clients' souls and auras, to leave them feeling fresh and clearly tuned. However, it was discouraging to see that the deeper issues could reappear in people's lives, whether in the same way, or in a slightly different form.

So, I learned to go deeper and to seek the beliefs that were founded in experiences from their present and past lives. I would help clients release the emotional and mental energies that were stuck and so bring about a deeper level of healing. Still, the deepest issues often reappeared again and again. Seeking the cause, I discovered soul contracts, or deep agreements, which can be created before and during incarnation or passed down through our parents' lineage, either genetically or socially. I learned to invite those contracts to be rewritten or cleared, and people would seem better for a while, but many issues continued to reemerge in their lives.

Finally, through a student of mine, I learned to recognize the "keepers" of the contracts, which are little energy magnets programmed to create and recreate the experiences that are contracted for. So, even when I erased the energy block that created the problem, the keeper recreated it in accordance with its contract.

With this knowledge, I was able to clear the keepers, too, which worked great, but then some issues began to show up again in new and more potent forms. I came to understand these potent forms as "backup systems." I learned that when the blocks, which are oppositional forces in our lives, were created, they had a purpose. They were designed to challenge our souls to grow and build the soul muscles and qualities that a particular facet of God needed to be developed as a human capacity. When these soul-developing systems were created, it was difficult to know exactly how much challenge would be required to get the job done, so in case the original version was too easy, backup systems of increasing potency and challenge were put in place to provide all the oppositional force needed to build the necessary soul qualities. There are usually eleven backup systems, making twelve versions all together! This process is similar to increasing the weight on our workout machines. Once we get used to five-pounds, we add more weight for more of a challenge.

All of these discoveries gave me a great deal of respect for the fact that our facet of God that lives within us has goals for our human lives, which from a human perspective we don't always willingly participate in! Any resistance we have to growing in the needed direction only increases the discomfort of the process. So, as a healer working with these contractual processes, I have learned to be very respectful of the higher intention that created them. Working from a high enough perspective, a healer can often help people to get what they need out of their contracts with a lot less stress and discomfort. Contracts can often be rewritten or the backup systems cleared when a person no longer needs quite so much opposition. But where the stress and discomfort are still needed, it is better to accept and work within that limitation than to try to clear it prematurely and get one of the backup systems on board! Once the need for the experience is fully satisfied, all versions can be cleared.

As we move into the new world, a lot of these old contracts based on opposition and pain are gradually being eliminated; in their place we are receiving upgrades of our contracts, our bodies, and our souls. These higher vibration systems allow us to merge with higher and higher levels of consciousness and so cocreate with God in an easier and more satisfying manner. Earlier in this book, I used the analogy that life was like a pinball machine. Surely that's a painful way to be directed toward our goals! I like the new world process much more!

Mind Over Matter

Today, there is a popular spiritual belief that our minds create our reality. On a higher level, we could say this is true: the consciousness of God within us designs our experience, and since we are God in our deepest truth, we create our experience. But the "mind" (and that is ascending, so it is changing as I write this) that people are referring to is generally a lower focus responding to the lower half of Tipheret or the ego. The ego does help create the experiences we are contracted for, but it can't create anything enduring if it is contrary to our contracts. With conscious and deliberate focus, the mind can appear to move our experience in a different direction, but if that direction is not in harmony with the higher will contracted within our lives, it will ultimately falter and fall back to square one. That's okay. There are much better ways to get where we are going than by projecting it with our lower minds! This idea has been useful in pointing us in the direction of understanding that we can partner with God to create our experience. The reality, however, is both simpler and more complex.

Yesod is the seed of our experience. It is a matrix built of contracts entered into by our higher consciousness for the purposes of our soul development. The contractual matrix includes DNA and other hereditary factors and the experiences, thoughts, emotions, spiritual blocks, and other defining elements in our present and past lives. As Hod brings to focus the energy of life through us, it travels along the path of evolution into

Yesod. There it is formed according to the contractual matrix and prepared for planting on Earth as the seed of our experience. Earth grows that seed and we find ourselves confronted with experiences that will ultimately help our bodies and souls to grow into the vehicles that can house and reveal our own unique facets of God.

To change soul contracts, we have to fulfill their intentions, unless, through ascension, those intentions become unnecessary, which is happening increasingly. As a healer, I work with each client's soul across time within his or her current life, past life, and even future life to initiate learning, healing, and changes at the point in time where he or she will have the greatest impact on the soul's evolution. Working this way, contractual obligations can often be fulfilled, and once they are, their keepers and backup systems can be cleared. This frees the soul to experience new levels of learning and fulfillment. It is always a relief when the old problem stops showing up in our lives, and we can move on to something we like better!

The Qabalah ascension meditations in the chapter titled "Tools to Streamline Ascension" will help you clear outdated contracts and work through them as needed.

As we ascend into the new world, the old world process of soul development is accelerated and then ultimately upgraded to a whole new strategy of partnering with God. There is a new way of growing and being that is coming on stage in our lives and in our world. This change is actively underway as of the writing of this book, and will continue over the next twenty to thirty years for those who are ascending into the new world during this phase of the process. It will take longer for those who are contracted to continue in the old world for a while yet. Each soul will shift at the pace that is scheduled for them individually. There will be a wide window of opportunity that allows everyone to come on board at the right time for them. Everyone will ultimately ascend, but for some it will be lifetimes yet. There are other options for them, and they are right and purposeful too.

The Archangel for the sphere of Yesod is Archangel Gabriel

Now inward to Man's inner being
There pours itself the wealth of senses.
There finds itself the spirit of worlds
As mirrored in the human eye

– *Rudolf Steiner,* the Calendar of the Soul

Sphere 10

The Mirror

Malkuth – Under Foot – The Physical World, Earth

The seed of Yesod is planted into the mirror of the physical world, which is called Malkuth on your Tree of Life. The unconditionally loving Mother Earth grows that seed into experiences perfectly designed to mature your soul so that it can become a vehicle for your own Eternal Divine Self to self-actualize within the world. Your experiences in this lifetime reflect back to you the opportunities you need in order to grow into the person you are destined to become.

No two people in the same time and place have the exact same experience. If siblings or twins compare notes about their childhood, it is likely that their perspectives on the experience are very different. There is no point in blaming our parents, the state of our finances, our country, or any other people or circumstances for the challenges we face in our lives. Each person we meet is an actor contracted to be on the stage of our lives, and each circumstance is a stage setting designed by our higher consciousness to give us the experience we need. Our job is to learn to work within that set of limitations. Once we have gained what we need, the restrictions will pass.

Circumstances are designed to focus our light within our lives. The focus and effort required to succeed in life works to anchor individual facets of God into the world, in order to actualize God's whole potential here. They build qualities within our soul bodies that become the structures that allow our unique facet of the One to function with increasing success in the world. Once that is accomplished, limitation will be a non-issue. We are eternal, safe, and unbreakable. We will surmount whatever challenges we face to arrive in a better place in due time. We are capable of achieving what is needed where we are. What is needed, however, may look different to our human selves in the midst of the experience than to the higher part of us that created the experience.

It is also part of the contractual journey when we or those around us appear to be stuck or indulging in damaging or bad behaviors. Sometimes there can be a lot of judgments made about these behaviors, and yet, when the need for them is fulfilled, they will change. People will wake up and decide to do things differently, and once that has happened, nothing will stop them from realizing their potential.

Sometimes people seem to play roles within their families or societies that are self-sacrificing or self-damaging. There is something for their souls to gain from the experience, however.

For instance, some children seem to manifest all the shadow elements of their families that the others cannot see within themselves. There are those who seem to live only for others, neglecting their own needs. In these situations and others, we can be sure that these people are fulfilling a contract for the development of the soul qualities they need.

> *The mirror of life reflects so finely*
> *That only when we are past our own distortions*
> *Can we fully see the perfection of it all.*

> -Penny Golden, publisher, *Body Mind Spirit Guide* magazine

Interpreting the purpose behind the experiences of life is a lot like dream interpretation. Life experience is subtle, personal, and symbolically precise, just like a dream. From the perspective of our higher selves, life as we know it *is* a dream. It is a dream that includes separation from God and usually elements of loneliness and suffering. Within this dream, though, we experience love, beauty, and so many amazing relationships and interrelationships that it is a deeply meaningful experience. It seems real to us, and because of that we grow through it. But because it is a dream, once we awaken to our more conscious state of being, the pain and suffering quickly fade while the wisdom, beauty, and love are carried onward into our waking existence—or in other words, our increasingly ascended state, as gifts to help us on our way.

If we want to change our experience within the physical world, we need to look beyond the form of things to the level of cause. Understanding the purpose behind our experience can help us work to fulfill our contracts, so that we can move on to the next experience life has planned, rather than recreating the same problems over and over, as often happens.

An inner alarm clock goes off when our souls are ready to awaken to God consciousness. This sets us on the whole new journey of ascension. Once we awaken, the old experience begins to pass away as the new experience is being born. This happens at the level of the individual, society, and the planet. This is a good thing, although if we are looking at the death of the old world experience, it can seem terrible, as though everything we once relied on is falling apart. If we focus on the awakening element and the increased presence of enlightenment and wholeness within our experience, we will find it a joy.

The planet Earth is a soul as well. Her body is going through a death and rebirth too. Her soul is awakening to her unity with God and her rightful, conscious place within the solar system, the universe, and beyond.

Vision – Mother Earth – 2010

It is a lovely, unusually warm November morning. I am in my garden. The apple trees have dropped their leaves and apples; the maple leaves have turned red and gold and fallen. Everything has been cleaned up, bagged, and sent to be composted. The ferns are mostly gone, and only the grape vine, evergreens, and lamium ground cover are still green. I see some tiny purple flowers still growing on the lamium. I am impressed by the powerful life force within this tiny plant that can produce flowers this late in the season.

From deep within my heart I speak to the flower and thank it for bringing its beauty into my life. As if in response to my communication, a huge soul presence begins to bloom out of the tiny purple flower.

It is clear energy with a shimmering opalescence and hint of rose. I am amazed by its strength. As I feel its loving energy deep within my heart and soul, I recognize it as the spirit of Mother Earth.

With my spiritual vision and feelings, I become aware of many layers of reality. It is as though the world is a room full of mirrors, where everything is reflected endlessly over and over in every direction, and then the reflections suddenly fall away, leaving only one layer of reflection—the present experience. All is suddenly quiet and open for a new birth. I know that what I am seeing is the breaking down of old world energy structures, in preparation for bringing in the new world experience.

Now the beautiful, feminine voice of Earth speaks as though from within me and all around me at the same time. She tells me not to worry. She is aware of how sad I have been about the animals, plants, and life forms that appear to be dying off and leaving the planet. She wants me to know that they are all being reborn within the new world. While they appear to die off, they really have gone ahead to prepare the new world for the rest of us.

This helps me to understand why so many of those who are leaving seem to be the wisest and best of us, like the whales and the ancient trees among others.

Thank you, Mother Earth, for your message and your undying love. I am honored to be here in the world to experience and help with this transition, but most especially I am honored that you have given me this vision and these words that comfort me so much. I'll share them with others, so that they will know not to worry and can move forward in life with greater confidence and joy.

The Archangel for the sphere of Malkuth is Archangel Sandalphon

Part III

WAVES OF CHANGE

Hitting the Bottom
of the Tree

As I mentioned earlier, the Qabalah, or Tree of Life, is holographic rather than linear. Each sphere contains a whole Tree of Life within itself, and each sphere within that sphere likewise contains a whole tree. Like a room with mirrors on all walls, the journey of the Qabalah is reflected everywhere we look. So it would be simplistic to think of the journey of the Path of the Lightning Bolt as a one-time experience. It is a complex journey taking place on every level of our soul simultaneously, each part of us growing at its own pace. Our conscious selves may arrive at a level of evolution that is far more enlightened than our unconscious selves, just as one person in the world ascends ahead of another. It is sufficient for us to focus on whatever element of growth and ascension is demanding our attention at any given time, and when we do, the Qabalah can help us understand what is occurring and how to work with it. This helps to explain why sometimes we feel and act enlightened and sometimes quite the opposite! We must be kind to ourselves either way. We'll get there in due time! It has already been established in spirit that we will. Now it just waits to be done in form.

Now that we've journeyed together along the Path of the Lightning Bolt to the bottom of the Tree of Life, let's review what we have done so far:

1. We began in **Kether** with our origin and true identity as part of the One that is the Source of Life.
2. I shared a memory of helping to sing the world into being as angels in **Chokmah,** where the One gave birth to the Cosmic Christ, the first individual soul.
3. In **Binah,** the Cosmic Christ conceived life forms independent of the One within the Mother God, initiating our journey of incarnation to build individual soul bodies through the illusory experience of separation.

Transitioning through the womb of Binah, we left behind our purely spiritual origins and experienced a primal birth trauma in **Daat,** finding ourselves separate for the first time.

4. We entered a physical body and learned about relationships and survival in the sphere of **Chesed**, where we also had a vision of personal destiny.
5. In **Geburah,** we found an inner drive calling us to make independent choices and moving us toward our destiny.
6. In **Tipheret** we met our Inner Wisdom and the potential for self-mastery of both our spiritual and our ego selves.
7. In **Netzach** we felt the chaotic but creative force of nature within us: instinct, emotion, and passion.
8. In **Hod** we learned of the mind's ability to focus that power into specific directions, ideally guided by our Inner Wisdom.

9. In **Yesod** we saw the energy of our lives being defined by our contracts, heredity, and unconscious beliefs— creating the seed of our experience.
10. In **Malkuth** we realized how those contracts give birth to our experience in the physical world.

So here we are, a part of the One Source of Life, having traveled through the journey of creation along the Path of the Lightning Bolt to build a soul body that can house our potential. We are both the creator and the creation, and we have come to an exciting transition. Having traveled as far into separation as was needed in order to develop a soul body and learn to function within it, we are ready to take the next step. Now we begin to merge physical body and soul with our true, unique, and eternal facet of God a little bit more each day.

Following the Path of the Lightning Bolt, life on earth has reached the end of the old evolutionary contracts. We have finished what we started and are ready to begin something new. We still have some cleanup and reorganizing to do, but we are already in the ascension phase of our evolution, which will bring us increasingly into union with our true selves. While there are those still working with the old contracts, the thrust of evolution on planet Earth is moving on.

Here is an analogy that describes this process: Until now we have been swimming downward from the light of the sun, the symbolic source of our being, going deeper and deeper into the sea of unconsciousness, which represents created experience. The lower we went, the denser our energy became until we forgot that we were beings of light and truth. Having reached the bottom of the sea, the darkest place in this vast experience, we now are turning back toward the light. Placing our feet on the bottom, we push off toward the surface. It's a long swim up, but easier than going down, because our spirit longs for the light of our truth and will carry us up until we break the surface into the light that we remember from our beginning so long ago. Along the way we will shed the weight of darkness and suffering that has pushed us to the bottom of the sea. As we arise, we become lighter and clearer and reclaim more and more of our true spirit until we find ourselves reunified with the light of our source.

Through the ascension process, our bodies and souls become increasingly light and clear until the true spirit that created our journey of life is able to awaken within us on every level. Each step of this reunification will bring us a deeper sense of belonging, purpose, ease, and satisfaction with life. We will also go through the process of letting go of the old, and finally finishing the contracts we've been unable to finish before—both of which can make the journey bumpy at times. If we release our fear and surrender to the change, we can ride the waves to the shore of the new world. I have tools to help us surf!

First though, I want to discuss a number of points that will help us understand the process of ascension and how it will impact our lives and our world. Some of these effects are positive and some are challenging. The challenges are transitional, but significant. The benefits will be ongoing and will increase exponentially over time.

Enlightened Souls within Our Seas

It is a great privilege and gives me such hope to discover—and then partner with in my spiritual healing and ascension work—enlightened beings living within other life forms on Earth. It requires an intuitive heart and mind to understand and communicate with those who are so different from us, and many people miss out on the opportunities they present for our edification and growth.

Of the many creatures within our seas, there are three types of creatures I currently work with who carry high levels of spiritual awareness. Each of them has massive direct lines of connection to God that allow them to anchor higher consciousness into the world and facilitate ascension on Earth. I will list them beginning with those I have worked with least and finish with those I have worked with the most.

Dolphins

Dolphins live in a state of unity with the One Source, which keeps them mostly free of fear, enabling them to be happy, friendly, forgiving, free, playful, and powerful! In my work with the ascension process, they carry healing that is done in one aspect of creation further and further into other levels of creation, multiplying the effect of the healing in areas ready to receive it. Because they are an incarnation of the Cosmic Christ, which exists as a seed waiting to be awakened within all of us, they carry an energy of unconditional love, joy, and forgiveness. One of my students who was blessed to swim with dolphins told me that they taught her to love herself for the first time, to find joy, and to trust life. I know I saw a great shift in her, and I'm sure there are many who have experienced this gift in similar ways. I know they do more than this, but I haven't been brought further into relationship with them yet to learn more. I look forward to this when I am invited to do so!

Sea Turtles

In some Native American stories, our world was created on the back of a turtle. The turtle is a very ancient creature, with profoundly enlightened consciousness that extends into the cosmos well beyond Earth. I met a sea turtle on a trip to Hawaii while snorkeling. She was remarkably friendly, and I am told this is typical of these wonderful creatures!

During the Ascension Support class that followed my Hawaii trip, a student asked if I had a message from the sea turtle that I could share with them, and I had to admit that I had been too busy to listen! Immediately, as I was answering her, the spirit of the sea turtle spoke to me and asked to meet with me in a healing meditation for the planet. I heard the sea turtle as a clear voice, which is different from listening to whales, whose communication feels to me like their sonar is resonating through the tissues of my body. Her voice was smooth and light, with a gentle kindness and dignity; her words were gracious and cordial. She felt grandmotherly. She told me I could invite one or two guests to meet with her.

When two fellow planetary healers and I met with the sea turtle, she got right down to business. As she spoke, we felt the presence of large schools of fish and other sea creatures supporting and reinforcing her message. It was clear they were very concerned about the issues to be addressed. The sea turtle explained that the toxic levels of bacteria in the oceans, lakes, rivers, and air stimulated people to greedy behavior and to use money in hateful ways.

The sea turtle's perspective on this issue was very interesting to us. I would think that people's hateful behavior and greed have prompted them to make choices that create conditions in which toxic bacteria grows out of control. The sea turtle's perspective was that the toxic bacteria create poor behaviors in people. As we worked to bring healing to these issues, the validity of her approach became clearer to us and has helped us in subsequent healing work with the waters, as well as with trees, humans, and animals who all can suffer greatly from toxic bacteria.

The sea turtle directed us to work with many types of toxic bacteria. Many things were brought into greater balance while we were in her presence. We cleared a significant amount of toxicity in the water and air as well in people's emotional and mental states. We were asked to assist by inviting the Higher Power to take authority over the influence of money, hatred, and toxic bacteria on people and all water on Earth. We sensed how these negative energies significantly increased the force within people that tends toward war.

Inviting God or the Higher Power to take authority over problems and old world energy systems like those mentioned above is a significant step for ascension. The old world journey created blocks to our connection with the consciousness of God, although God lives within all of life. It takes a conscious being in a physical body to request that healing and change occur. When the one requesting the healing is grounded into his or her body and the Earth and simultaneously connected to God, then the Higher Power can act directly, to ascend the life force and the energy structures of thought, emotion, body, and aura. This allows the problems and energy blocks to heal. The increased unity between Higher Power and the created world creates wholeness and well-being.

Within a week of our work with the sea turtle, our team of healer and ascension workers was guided to work with the toxic algae that had created a dead space within Lake Erie. Much of what we learned working with the sea turtle was relevant to our work for the lake.

It was obvious to me that somehow the disease of the lake was related to an energy of war, although it wasn't until one of our healing partners mentioned the Indian Wars that it became clear to me how it related. We were guided to forgive a curse that had been placed on the lake by an individual as a result of that war, reassuring that discarnate soul that they are—and have always been—loved by God, and helping their spirit return to God. We helped release a lot of toxic emotions and souls that had died but had not yet crossed into the light from that experience. As this occurred, we saw the algae clearing, like a cloud lifting and dissipating. We saw and felt the pure spirit and power of the lake reemerge and grow rapidly in light and beauty. It became like a spring of true spiritual wholeness filling the lake, the surrounding region, and expanding into the rivers and ground water as well. There was a sweet smell, and the crystalline, sparkling energy was obviously Holy Spirit, but at the same time uniquely Lake Erie.

Lake Erie is an amazingly beautiful soul! I remember her unique beauty of spirit from when I was just a toddler visiting my grandmother's cottage. This amazing lake healed herself once when she was terribly poisoned from industrial waste in the 1960s, before the Clean Water Act was finally passed, which brought changes allowing her soul to reclaim and heal her body. Now she is healing even more deeply from the dark despair of the Indian Wars, which created a dead spot within her body that had grown for a long time. Thank you, Lake Erie, for your great love, courage, beauty, forgiveness, and strength! And thank you, sea turtle, for your guidance and love.

Recently algae has been increasing again in Lake Erie; which alerted me to meditate on the situation. I was shown how she is focusing the healing and ascension process for all water, planet-wide. Algae is a vehicle that the Higher Power is using to collect anger and hatred which has built up through all lifetimes here on earth. It will ultimately be released into God's care to heal and ascend. The spirit of Lake Erie in partnership with God are directing this process for us. This higher-level task she has chosen to do requires her to experience toxic algae within her own waters, until it can all be fully embraced and processed through the energy of the Higher Power. This will help all of us on earth ascend since our bodies are largely made up of water!

Our earlier healing work with Lake Erie and the Indian Wars helped to initiate this healing and ascension for the whole worlds' water. The vision of her beauty and light growing and radiating through the surrounding rivers and ground water is the promise of the ascended state for our lakes, rivers and oceans. It already exists in spirit and truth, so we can trust the process it takes to finally manifest the experience physically through ascension.

We know that algae grow out of balance because of toxic chemicals used by industry and other poor human choices. And as Sea Turtle told us, toxic algae make humans behave in hateful ways. However, that does not diminish the value of this toxic state, which allows deeper healing to occur by collecting anger and hatred to be cleared by God. This facilitates the ascension process for all of us, and shows how everything works together for the greater good! It is such a relief to know this, for someone like myself who is intensely sensitive to the health of our world.

Whales

Anyone who has ever seen a whale in the wild has sensed the presence of great power, wisdom, and infinite love. I'd like to introduce these beings from a spiritual perspective to help us understand more about who they really are.

Several years ago in Hawaii, I wanted to go on a whale watching cruise to see the humpback whales that winter there and raise their young in the warm water. I had heard about the role that whales and dolphins play in helping us ascend to a higher level of consciousness in partnership with the Creator, but I hadn't explored this for myself.

I saw the whales spouting off shore at sunrise on my first day on Oahu. I felt awed and excited by the huge plumes of water that they shoot from their blowhole. I was told that when a whale spouts, the plume consists of approximately one cup of water and a very strong blast of air rising high enough to be seen for miles!

On the day of the whale cruise, I went into a meditative state and asked to connect with a whale. Immediately, I perceived the eye of a whale that seemed very close to me. I felt welcomed and assured that we would meet on the cruise. I was reminded that I was supposed to work with the whales in my healing practice to assist the healing and evolution of people and all life on the planet. It felt as though I was beginning a new and deeper adventure in my work.

We saw many whales on our cruise. Two pods swam with us for a long time, and we saw adults and little ones very close. It was exciting and joyful to feel their intelligence, playfulness, and love. One of the mother whales was clearly the individual I had met in my meditation. Her powerful love stays with me to this day.

During the two years following that trip, I visited with the whales in spirit and was guided to work much more deeply with the healing of the planet and all who live on it. I was asked by a particular whale to do a series of advanced healing classes for my graduate students in which we developed tools and skills to assist us in our individual and collective evolution to a state of unity and unconditional love. If you listen to the news, you may think that these ideas are unrealistic, but when you listen to your heart and your soul, you will know that we are well on our way. And *that* is *exciting*!

I was able to return to Oahu for a winter visit and again saw the whales off shore, spouting and this time breaching, fins flying through the morning air off shore at dawn! When planning the trip, I had called the cruise line and was told that they had only three whale sightings during the season so far. I tuned in with my whale friends and was told that if I went on the cruise they would come, so I scheduled it. The boat cruises the length of Honolulu Bay, where the humpbacks come to enjoy the warm water, which is easier for their babies to handle. Amazingly, the adults don't eat the whole season, since their food source is unavailable in Hawaii's warm waters.

When the day arrived, our boat cruised the full length of Honolulu Bay without a sign of whales. I began to feel discouraged and to doubt my spiritual information. I was standing at the front of the boat as it turned away from the bay toward the deeper ocean when I was the first guest on board to see a whale spout directly ahead of us, three or four miles away. As we neared the area where the whale had spouted and we didn't see it, I began to worry. Then I realized that directly ahead of us was a cloud shaped exactly like a leaping humpback whale. It was as if to say: "Don't worry, I'm coming!" About ten minutes later, we saw a young male whale flap his tail at us! He followed us for about an hour, surfacing every four minutes or so, showing us the beautiful arch humpbacks make when they breach. The shipboard naturalist commented on how extraordinary this was, since ordinarily they surface only every twenty minutes.

When it was time to go inside for lunch, I sent a message of thanks to the whale for coming and being such good company. While I was dishing up my meal, he surfaced right outside the window of the serving line, and when I went to my table on the other side of the boat; he swam under the boat and surfaced right in front of our table! I tuned in again and felt such a strong and exuberant wave of love from him. He told me that he wanted me to know that I am loved and that he came there to see me. I felt extremely blessed, grateful, and joyful. What a gift!

Later I checked in with the young whale to see if he had returned to his pod. No, he was off to another island to support another group of whale lovers so that they would know they were loved, too. I asked him how the whales were going to handle the climate changes Earth is undergoing. He told me that they would adapt and that he is one of a new generation of whales that can handle the climate changes more easily. I was thrilled!

I have learned that whales are an incarnation of the Divine Beings who helped to create our world and who are working to help it ascend into a more enlightened state. As we get to know the whales in our hearts and our souls, we find that they are also teaching us how to be a part of that ascension process. They remind us who we really are, cocreators with God, learning how to work with the Creator to give birth to a world that we will really enjoy.

Whale Vision

It is just a few months after returning from my second visit to Hawaii, and I am meditating in preparation for my workday. Unexpectedly, a blue whale comes to me; she is massive and her touch is gentle but firm. She leads me through the ocean, and I follow in her wake to the ocean floor where the light is so dim I can just see her pale color glowing. As she lands, sand and debris rise up around her, and she leaves her body as in death. My soul cries out—no! But before I can get upset, she speaks to me with great love. She has been here for a very long time in one whale form or another, and now that I am here, she can leave. I sense the passing of responsibility from her to me, and it makes me wonder how she expects me to do this job. But I am here, and I am willing.

I am still in touch with the soul of blue whale, and while I have hesitated to print this part of my story, it is with her insistence that I place it here. She says she knows the importance of this book. I am grateful to have a role in the ascension of our world and honored by her trust in me.

In constant self-creating
Soul-Being comes to self-awareness,
The spirit of worlds is striving forth
In self-cognition new-enlivened
And shapes from darkness of the soul
Self-senses fruit of will

– Rudolf Steiner, *the Calendar of the Soul*

Death and Rebirth

I notice that after a time of great challenge, a soul can seem born anew. A person may find that he or she has grown exponentially through the experience, emerging ready to begin life from an entirely new place.

It is extremely helpful to maintain a focus on the new world energy and the positive direction that life is taking, so that we can more easily let go of our old world identities and move with the changes needed in order to give birth to our new world selves. Watching or reading the news presents many opportunities for us to struggle with the old world experience, which may keep us identified with and stuck in the old world state. The media make more money when they sensationalize and get us stirred up about things; that's their job. If we choose to watch the news, it is a good idea to invite God to be present with the world's problems and to awaken within each situation when the time is right, to help those issues to resolve for everyone's highest good. That invitation opens the door for things to work out more gently, and it can help us release our concerns more easily and to stay focused on strengthening our new world experience.

In order for the new world to be born, the old world must pass away. Much of that passing away, and the grief of that passing, will be muted by the birth of the new world that happens simultaneously. When we are focused in our new world experience, the birthing of the new world buoys us and helps us to release the old.

I am continually reassured by the memory of my vision, discussed in the chapter on Malkuth, in which Mother Earth made it clear that all life forms which appear to become extinct will be reborn in new world bodies and that nothing will be lost in this transition except our suffering and separation.

This knowledge helps me to surrender my resistance when it appears that so much of what I love in the natural world is dying and so many people are suffering. It also helps with the passing of people who are transitioning out of my life as I ascend, or out of the old world by dying rather than ascending. The grief of these changes can be experienced and released more quickly, because I understand that life is eternal, and letting go is only a temporary stage. All the people and life forms I love will be reborn in the new world experience in due time. Aware of the suffering we have all endured in so many lifetimes through our old world journey, I am willing to surrender to the death aspect of ascension, so that we can experience a better reality in the new world.

I don't like the death part of the journey, so I do a great deal of healing work to smooth the transition for people and the planet, and I feel reassured that my work makes a difference. This helps me a lot.

A visit to the redwood forests of Northern California initiated a series of visions and dreams. They helped me again to face the death of the old, and to see how I am being taught to assist the Essence of Truth of God within all things to awaken within the creation and birth the new world experience. Helping in this type of way becomes very natural as we ascend into partnership with the Essence of Truth of God within ourselves.

Vision of Redwood Tree 1

I am leaning with my hands on the giant trunk of the tallest standing redwood tree in Founder's Grove, California, called Founder's Tree. As my cheek rests against its bark, I feel comforted by its great strength and maturity. I am quickly drawn to look upward, as though through the body of the tree, seeing with the tree's own vision. I see stars and feel the circling power and pull of the planets and the universe. I feel very much aware of the benevolent power present everywhere and of my place (the redwood tree's place) within the All That Is.

I hear the word remember and am then quickly returned to my human self-awareness and my ordinary consciousness.

Redwood Tree, Meditation 1

Later, sitting in meditation, I returned to the Founder's Tree in spirit and continued my conversation with this two-thousand-year-old redwood friend. Again, I felt the word remember and the awareness came that the universe is eternal and there is much loving support and truth always there for us.

I went deeper still into that word and all of the feelings and information that came with it. It was a very potent single word, holding a whole lot of truth within it, and I wanted to receive everything it had to say.

I was amazed and impressed by such an ancient perspective and unswerving confidence in life that this tree had, a feeling of great benevolence and the ongoing experience of life, as well as comfort and confidence in the goodness of all things.

I asked the tree about ascension. It assured me that we are well into the process of ascension and that there is no question it is happening. I also asked if it would still be alive in a hundred years, and if so, what the world would be like? It said that it would be on Earth and that the new world would be a much more alive and happy place to live! I looked ahead five hundred years, which to these trees is not such a long time. I could sense that the world would be filled with much more light and would exist on a higher plane of being. I love the way these huge trees bridge the changes in our world with strength and ease. I feel so grounded and whole when I experience their consciousness!

Redwood Tree, Meditation 2

I feel drawn to invite the spirit of the redwood tree into myself, in a way similar to merging with a power animal in the shamanic tradition. I feel I have a lot to learn and gain through this process.

I surrender my focus of human self as I open to the experience of what I perceive as my own redwood tree, which is quite distinct from the Founder's Tree in energy and personality. I feel amazingly tall and deep and open within, aware again of the stars and the universe, of immense strength, power, and permanence. I also feel a great joy, like returning to a place I once called home.

My body and aura feel a bit overwhelmed by this amount of power! I have to return to normal awareness after only a minute or even less. Wow!

Dream

In the wee hours of the following morning after my second redwood tree meditation, I am on the verge of awakening, yet still asleep. My soul feels itself in the presence of the redwood trees, and suddenly there are good size segments of fallen redwood trees lying sideways and being served up to me on small plates, like eggrolls in a Chinese Restaurant!

I awaken and wonder ... What?

Lying in bed and contemplating the eggroll-type redwood tree dream, I realize that I need to digest my redwood tree wisdom in smaller portions than merging with the whole tree!

Vision of Redwood Tree 2

Lying in bed, I welcome the integration of the first of the pieces of redwood tree.

I feel immense heat, dryness, and high winds and see dust and fire in the redwoods.

I pull myself up and out of this vision and exclaim, "No!"

I am reminded of the smoke-filled valleys we drove through on our first evening in the redwoods. We were told the smoke was from forest fires burning in southern Oregon, not far from where we were.

Willing myself to relax and surrender to trust, knowing that everything will work out to be fine in the long run, I ask what I am being shown.

I am told that many of the redwoods will eventually burn in the old world, but enough will remain standing to bridge the old and new worlds. This is part of releasing the old world experience so we can transition into the new.

I am shown the new world redwood forest from the vantage of being halfway between the old and new worlds. It is like looking through broken glass; I can see both images perfectly but with a little different focus, as though each is on one side of a crack in the glass. The new world is above the old and partially superimposed on it. If I duck down, I can see the old, and the fires raging; if I look up I can see the new world in essence, as though the trees were made of spiritual substance, both white and clear.

The word remember comes to me again and I realize that I am supposed to remember what it is like to be a redwood tree, so that I may help the new world redwood trees recreate themselves on that higher level of being.

When I open my heart to help with that, I suddenly perceive miles and miles of redwood trees in the new world, fully developed, healthy, and whole. I am treated to a marvelous feeling of strength, joy, and full-powered redwood in all its glory!

Endings and Beginnings

In writing this book, all I desire is to share with you the joy and blessing of ascension, but there is no avoiding that the old world is passing away within us and our world; this is part of the journey of rebirth. My job as a healer and teacher is to find ways to minimize the trauma of the death of the old and smooth the journey into rebirth—but not so much that people miss the opportunities they need during this transition. My Weekly Word for Healing & Ascension Blog, Monthly Ascension Support Classes, Healer and Ascension Certification Course, private healing treatments, and the Graduate Group, which meets to assist with the planetary and cosmic ascension process, are having a significant impact, making the process easier for all. However, most people are aware of the changes occurring on the planet, which include global warming, the degradation of the environment, the destruction of the habitat for wild creatures, and the challenges that all living things, including humans, are facing. We have all, no doubt, wondered how it will all end.

Well, the good news is that it is not so much an end as a beginning. We are being reborn, and so is the world—at a higher level where we will realize our true potential and release suffering to live in a greater state of unity and fulfillment.

When you perceive the death phase of the journey, remember to look for the birth that is its opposite and its compliment in the new world. It will always be there.

I have learned that the world doesn't need to heal to ascend; but that in ascending she will become new and whole in every way! Healing is needed for humans to release the traumas of our past so we can harvest the gifts from our experiences and ascend. However, nature doesn't require that same process; she is ready to ascend whenever the green light is given from the One. Much of the natural world is holding pace with humans during our healing and ascension, providing opportunities we require at each step along the way. As a planetary healer and ascension worker, I find the problems that I am asked to help with seem primarily opportunities to release human karma and increase our unity with all of life. Then the natural world ascends a step and receives healing because of it. For lots of great stories about ascension and the natural world, visit my Weekly Word for Healing and Ascension Blog www.spiritualhealers.com/blog.

Letting Go of Baggage

On our journey of evolution in the old world, we have taken on layer upon layer of weight and darkness that have forced us further from the unity that is our truth. This state of separation was maintained during all of our lifetimes and forced us to function as individuals, rather than all One Being. Now that we have learned to function independently, we are beginning to shed that burden of darkness and the pain and suffering associated with it.

There are a couple of ways to shed that old baggage. One is to leave this body behind completely and be reborn into the new world in the future, where the new bodies and energy systems will be light and easy to live within. Many souls will choose this path over the coming years and when they pass away, they have good things ahead of them. Some souls in this group will collect darkness while they are in their current life in the form of psychological problems, self-destructive behaviors, or extremely traumatic experiences. When they die, they will carry that darkness into the light, easing the burden for everyone else. Their journey can teach us a hard lesson to learn: to love unconditionally and not judge, but to trust the process of life and its deeper purposes. When we see people making dark or destructive choices, or living through great hardship, it is likely they are taking temporary steps to accomplish a greater good.

The other way we can shed old baggage is to ascend while in a physical body. This exciting choice gives us a front row seat for the transformation of the planet! It also helps raise the vibration of the Earth and all life forms on it. As we ascend, we let go of the emotional, mental, spiritual, and physical blocks and habits of suffering that have been the norm, not only for this lifetime, but all others as well. Each time a soul shifts further into the new world, it paves the way for others, making it easier for them to release those old ways of being. Many of us here on earth are in the process of ascending and have been increasingly doing so for some time. Those who continue to ascend while in the physical body may live exceptionally long lives, enjoying increasing unity with their own truth and light, until they have finished everything they desire to do here and choose to move on to other dimensions and experiences. Transitioning out of a present life from within the new world state will not be death, but like a step into another room in the created universe. That has always been the case for the soul and spirit, but in our old world experience the body has had to be left behind to die and decay, so the soul could be free to move on, unencumbered by the lower energies of the body that have not been able to return into spirit with us. In the ascension process, the body will increasingly be brought to a high enough vibration to find union with the soul and spirit. Once this occurs sufficiently, people are able to bring their bodies with them into the next experience of life, rather than leaving them behind in death.

Eve Wilson

Where We Have Been Broken

In so many ways, life in the old world experience has broken us, but in so doing it has opened us to our higher potential. For many years, as a healer, I used to look at those wounded places in individuals and in our world as though they were a garment that had been torn, believing that healing would be like sewing the garment back together in the shape it had originally been—believing that to be the right shape. Through the ascension process, I learned that the broken places within us heal into a new shape, and the openings caused by the breaking become places where our true light can live more fully within us. What emerges is a new shape, but one that was designed from the beginning to hold our higher potential. This new shape welcomes the light of True Being to live more fully within our bodies, our souls, and our world.

The End of Sorrow – Ascension

In this new phase of evolution it may take some effort to wrap our consciousness around what is really available to us. The path we are now on leads to the end of sorrow, the healing of all that has been wrong in us and our world. Granted, this is not an instant fix, as there is work to do to let go of the old and realize the new. There are times when people with spiritual vision are allowed to look into the future, and it is made known to us that what we see is not, as is often the case, an optional destination where it may or may not happen; instead we are clearly told that what we are seeing is already a fact. This is the case with our ascension. There is no question that it is already completed on the highest planes of spirit. There is only the time it will take for us to experience that fact in our individual lives.

When we let go of old restrictions or wounds, there is a kind of grieving that goes with the release; this is a positive kind of grief that washes away the old and paves the way for the new. Because of this process, our ascension is not a straight-ahead emotional, mental, and physical lift. It is an up and down process, like a wave that intensifies, crests, and breaks, releasing us out of the old world and into a sense of freedom, increased strength, and wholeness. Then, over time, another wave builds, intensifying our experience again. Our acceptance of this process can ease our journey. Think of it as developing the skill of riding these waves of change into the new world experience.

In light that from the deeps of spirit
Weaves fruitfully in space
To open forth the god's creating;
In it appears the soul's own being
As widened into Being of Worlds
And resurrected
From narrow selfhood's inner might

– Rudolf Steiner, *Calendar of the Soul*

The Future

For a few reasons, it is hard to predict how long the ascension process will take us. First, each of us will do it on our own schedule. Second, the length of time predicted by spiritual sources has been getting shorter. Where the predictions below were first expected to take 50 years or more, now we are seeing that same amount of shift happening in approximately a thirty-year period! So things are far from set in stone. I don't want to hold onto what is predicted as it appears now, when we could be going more quickly! Alternately, if it takes a bit longer for some stages, maybe that would be necessary for something important to happen. I like to keep a very open mind about time. Third, there are many waves of change, and what looks good to us from here, will be seen as just the beginning of something much greater when we move farther along. We are only shown a bit at a time, like a puzzle: the more pieces we find and correctly place, the better we can see the finished picture. Our puzzle is only beginning to show us the bigger picture.

We are evolving toward an entirely new experience, and entering a new period of more than 340 million years of unity and cocreativity with God, during which time the Essence of Truth of God will become increasingly awake within all life forms. From what I see as of this writing, it looks like this: in ten years the new world will be stronger overall. There will still be many challenges, but having unloaded a vast quantity of old contractual burdens, life will be moving in a positive direction in every area of existence. We are currently in the cleanup stage, clearing the products of the old contracts in preparation for actualizing our new potential. In the process, we are gaining essential skills for what is to come. In twenty years our experience will be very new and greatly improved. We will have gained some skill in the process of cocreating with God, and will be moving forward with a thrust of light and positive energy. We will be over the hump; the death process of the old world will be nearly finished and the new world will be predominant, although still in very early stages. Life on Earth in thirty years will be vastly different and in all ways better. There will be a peace and gentleness that comes with trust and unity with God; the new world energy will be strongly characterized by the Holy Spirit, which will be a fertile foundation for new world life. In thirty-five years we will have reached a point where **all** souls on Earth will be 50 percent or more in unity with God within, which will be amazing!

These are predictions for the overall experience; individuals and groups may be ahead or behind in any of these areas as we go along. The process is exponential, so every movement forward prepares us for greater movement to come. But like a wave, there is up and down movement; each dip is really gathering energy to crest again at a higher level.

There is no need to resist the downward motion or struggle with individuals or groups who are not yet ready to move forward. Everything and everyone will move at the pace that is planned within their individual soul contracts. There is a reason for things to happen the way they do, and resisting this only takes us out of our own true direction. We must focus instead on riding each wave of growth as we experience it, and acknowledge that everyone is doing fine where they are. Even if some experiences seem negative and old world, it is what we need at the present time.

We will learn to respect each unique path. As we enter the new world we can let go of the idea of consensual reality. Each of us has our own experience in the new world. For each of us, our true selves are the creators of our experiences, and it is very personal. The collective picture will grow out of our many individual pictures, and it will be amazingly right. In order to enter that "just right" state, we have to stop trying to control others; doing so entwines us in their evolution and takes us off of our own path. It's okay if we do that, but we all eventually have to stop, so why not do so now? It makes life so much simpler when we do.

Steps to Ascension – Chakra Awakenings

How will you know you are ascending? What indicators do you have of these shifts? This chapter provides some landmarks and tuning forks to help you along the way.

The seven primary chakras within a person's aura are the interface between spirit and body that allow the soul to anchor into the physical world. Each of them supports essential elements of body, emotion, mind, and spirit. (See the Chakra Diagram at the end of this chapter.)

Within your soul contracts, there is a timer set to go off which awakens you to higher stages of evolution in consciousness, like an alarm clock awakening you in the morning. This timer reminds you that there is a whole lot more to you than you have known yet, and the dormant seed of your greater self begins to ripen within you. Using the chakra system described in this chapter, I will help you understand and support the birthing of your greater potential, demonstrating how it may unfold within yourself. This process may mirror changes you have already experienced, or, if it is different for you, it will give you an idea of what to expect. I use the term *God* here multiple times. Please feel free to use a different term if you prefer for that Oneness from which all life springs and the facet of that which exists within each created soul.

Try not to fit yourself into the structure presented; just be open to the different stages mentioned. They will happen in a unique way within you. You may be experiencing any one of the steps, or none at all. Your steps may be quite different. Or perhaps this information will be like a tuning fork that helps you come into harmony with the next step on your journey!

I am surprised to see how these stages unfold in the order they do. The process doesn't begin with the highest energy and work its way down or the lowest and work its way up. It begins deep within and finds its own unique way from there.

1. Navel Chakra – The awakening of desire within your instinctual self for what is real and true.

The first activation happens within the navel chakra; it is a deep, personal feeling within your unconscious will and instinctual self. It is a longing that causes you to seek beyond your prior experience for something absolutely true, essential, and real. It is a craving for more than what you have found in the world. It can't be satisfied by religion, books, relationships, sex, or mind-altering substances; it is not a concept or something you can learn. It is an innate awakening that can only be satisfied by connecting directly with the Divine present within yourself and all life. The ascension process will take you to that experience in a very personal and unique way.

Because this awakening happens within your deeply instinctual navel chakra, it holds the internal equivalent of a compass. Once your alarm clock goes off and this true desire awakens within you, you will bypass opportunities that would distract you from your clear direction and go straight to what is helpful to you. Your internal compass will guide you.

2. Crown Chakra – Accessing true source

Your awakening desire, combined with your internal compass, will lead you to connect directly to your true Divine Source through your crown chakra. This brings a flush of unconditionally loving energy into your body and aura. You remember that God is not something separate from you, but is who you are at the most profound levels of your being. God is where you come from. You experience a sense of belonging and purpose that goes far beyond this incarnation and that has always been present, although often hidden from your awareness.

3. Heart Chakra – Feeling positive, hopeful, trusting, lighter, ready for a new experience; Inner Wisdom.

Your heart opens and you begin to feel the essence of truth of God within your life. You experience a positive lightness and feeling of hope and trust that somehow everything will work out for the best. You see the world through new eyes, and you like it. You begin to feel engaged with a higher purpose, as though life has places to take you that you know you are going to love.

Go a little bit deeper, and you will find the still, clear place of your Inner Wisdom, which is most easily accessed through your heart chakra. This is the place where you have always known what is true and what is not. Your internal compass has always been active here. It is a core of the Cosmic Christ consciousness within your body; here lie the seeds of self-mastery and unconditional love.

4. Solar Plexus – Self-confidence and clarity of focus

You begin to identify more with the unique facet of God within you and less with what you do, who you thought yourself to be, or how the world sees you. This gives you a greater sense of self-confidence and clarity of focus. You find increased courage to be your most authentic self. You also find the ability to accept and trust that you are just what and who life needs you to be in each moment.

5. Root/Coccyx Chakra – Trust

You are more inclined to trust the essence of truth of God to provide for your life, and you stop struggling so hard to survive. You enter a state of grace in which you find yourself increasingly in the right places and fulfilling your purpose in the moment. What you need is available in just the right ways.

6. Third Eye – Seeing the world ascending

You learn to stop fighting with old world blocks. You are directed to the experiences in which there are openings for God to come into your life and awaken you to your true purpose. You become more patient when you feel blocks holding you back from within or resistance to your truth from without. You are able to bide your time and wait for the opportunity to ascend further. You understand that others ascend in their own time as well and can accept that for them.

7. Throat Chakra – Healing karmic wounds

Here you begin healing the deepest feelings of loneliness, separation, and sadness from your old karmic wounds and traumas. You are ready to let go and reclaim your oneness with Source, right here in your life and the world as it is. You are increasingly a bridge for God to act in the world, expressing truth and receiving love.

8. Four Other Chakras – Higher purpose

Four other chakras will become active within your energy field when you are ready to integrate higher levels of soul, which are a part of you, but haven't been able to express through your human self before. These chakras will become vehicles for the integration of your higher purpose within your life and through you to impact the world for good. Two chakras below your feet and two above your crown will eventually come into play when they are needed. I won't try to define them, but if you are paying attention, you can understand them through experience once they are functioning in your life. Trying to open them prematurely would create chaos in your energy field. Let them come to you in their own time.

Awakenings like these mentioned above aren't absolutes, but they are milestones or paradigm shifts within your soul and being. Once they occur, you have new inner resources available and an inner compass that helps you stay the course of your ascension process. You will still be a part of both the old and new worlds for a long time to come, so you may not always experience yourself at your best. That doesn't diminish the presence of your truth, so long as you eventually remember to return your focus to your new world self and release what isn't true for you any longer. You will encounter deeper and deeper levels of your truth as you ascend, and so these stages will occur multiple times in increasingly comprehensive ways.

Chakra Diagram

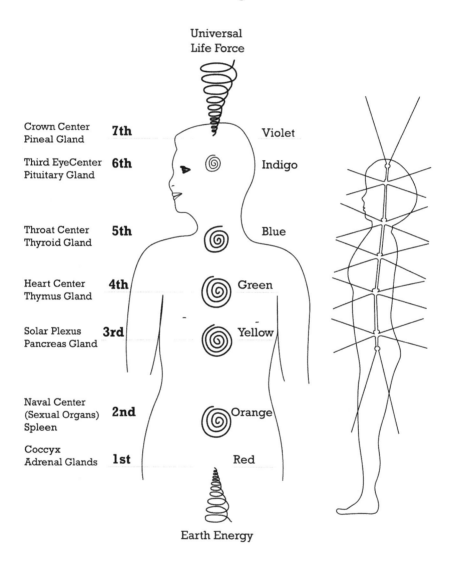

Universal Life Force

Crown Center
Pineal Gland — **7th** — Violet

Third EyeCenter
Pituitary Gland — **6th** — Indigo

Throat Center
Thyroid Gland — **5th** — Blue

Heart Center
Thymus Gland — **4th** — Green

Solar Plexus
Pancreas Gland — **3rd** — Yellow

Naval Center
(Sexual Organs)
Spleen — **2nd** — Orange

Coccyx
Adrenal Glands — **1st** — Red

Earth Energy

Part IV

SURFING

I can, enlivened new within
Now feel the width of my own being,
And filled with strength, shed rays of thought
From sun-might of the soul
Upon Life's riddles, solving them;
And lend fulfillment to those wishes
Whose wings were lamed before by hope

– Rudolf Steiner, the Calendar of the Soul

Tools to Streamline Ascension

As you ascend, you will increasingly merge into unity with the unique facet of divine consciousness that created your human self! Every aspect of your body and soul will gradually learn to identify with that true self. The other side of that shift is the release of things that have defined your self-identity in the past. Regardless of whether those self-defining traits are limitations or accomplishments, you will find a need to move beyond them to realize that you are more than all of them. Accomplishing this shift in identity and function affects every part of you, from the most enlightened aspect of soul to the tiniest particle of your body. This is the task of ascension.

Out of all the tools I have been given to assist with ascension, I have chosen those that can be shared effectively within this context. Although simple, this set of tools will help build an essential foundation to support your ascension.

The Essence of Truth – This may be the single most important tool for your ascension. In order to connect clearly, and at the highest level available to you at any given time, ask to connect with the Essence of Truth of any of the aspects of Self, God, Qabalah or spirit for any spiritual work you might do. This will help you bypass the lower spiritual energies and connect to the clearest and truest energies available. It will also help you to continually upgrade to higher levels of self and spirit connections as you ascend.

For example, ask to be connected with the Essence of Truth of your Inner Wisdom or the Essence of Truth of Archangel Michael, and so on. Then allow yourself to sense the clarity and truth within you. It isn't enough just to ask from your mind; follow the instructions in this chapter to work from your Inner Wisdom, and experience an actual shift in focus that carries a sense of rightness.

When you don't ask to be connected with the Essence of Truth, you may find that your spiritual connections can slip in and out of focus, or you may feel like you are trying to connect through a fog. The reason may be that your personal vibration has ascended to a higher level, but you are still trying to connect with your Inner Wisdom or spirit guides at a lower vibration where you used to function but no longer are. It is similar to needing a new prescription for your spiritual eyeglasses! Using the Essence of Truth request automatically upgrades you to the highest level at which you are currently functioning.

As you practice working with the Essence of Truth, you will learn to recognize more easily what is misleading or untrue in sprit, in your own consciousness, and in the world.

In the series of exercises in this chapter, I will give you more specific instructions for using this tool, but your use of it isn't limited by those tools. Anytime you talk to God or spirit guides or seek your Inner Wisdom, you can use the Essence of Truth.

Inner Wisdom – Your Inner Wisdom is a focus of enlightened consciousness within your human self. It may be found anywhere within you, but is most easily accessed through your heart chakra in the middle of your chest where it intersects with your pranic tube, a natural opening to your Higher Self and the Essence of Truth of God just behind your spine. This place of deep peace and balance is the natural home to your Essence of Truth, the eternal spark of the divine that you are. I call this your Inner Wisdom.

It is better to do your spiritual work from your Inner Wisdom rather than from your head. Your Inner Wisdom can integrate spiritual and physical energies to help you manifest your intentions in your daily life. When you work solely with your head or third eye chakra, the energy is not likely to be properly grounded. Instead of experiencing the real thing, you may create a mental or psychic image of it that can give you the impression that you've created something, but it won't quite ground into manifestation, doesn't last, or it is not the right thing. Your Inner Wisdom incorporates your third eye, mind and Higher Self and with practice your body and willpower. As these energies unite, you can make actual connections as intended and ground spirit into physical form, so that true changes occur in yourself and in your life.

It is in your Inner Wisdom that you recognize and discern the truth most clearly. The mind and third eye don't have that level of discernment; they are meant to collect data and focus it, but they don't possess the complex intuitive capability that your Inner Wisdom does. Your heart chakra, Inner Wisdom, and often your belly can incorporate most different levels of consciousness, including your deeper instinct, intuition, mind, and higher consciousness. This can bring you to a comprehensive awareness of what is true, what is false or simply misleading, and exactly what will work in any situation.

The mind can justify what it wants and, with the help of your third eye, can create convincing images that seem right and true, but they may not be quite right. Your Inner Wisdom is a trustworthy focus of self-awareness and truth. Inner Wisdom is most easily accessed initially through the heart chakra, but it can be accessed anywhere within you with practice. This part of you knows how to make use of the gifts of mind and third eye; they just need to be integrated into your Inner Wisdom.

Accessing Your Inner Wisdom

This is a way to access your Inner Wisdom, the sweet place within you from which you can learn to live from your truth and wholeness:

- Breathe into your body and give yourself an inner hug all the way down to your toes and up to the top of your head, welcoming your consciousness to be present within your body. This gets you home within your body.
- From there, breathe into your heart chakra in the middle of your chest, centering your consciousness there as

though this was the place where your mind, senses, and voice were actually located. Ask to access your new world heart chakra, which is a higher vibration focus of it.

- Allow your breathing to carry you backward into yourself, until you feel as far behind your spine as in front of it. There you will find a still place of inner clarity and peace. Center there and ask your Inner Wisdom to expand and fill you.

- Once you have found this sweet place within your soul, where you are one with the Divine, learn to live from that center. Invite your mind, senses, will, actions, and desires to be guided from this place. When you find yourself pulled by your mind or desires to act independently of your Inner Wisdom, you can stop and re-center on your Inner Wisdom. Then you can sense if these directions are right for you or if they are simply distractions. If it feels right, go with it; if not, wait until you sense what seems more right for you.

- In this aspect of yourself you have access to all wisdom and truth. When you are in need of answers or guidance, center in your Inner Wisdom, ask your questions, and wait for the answers to come to you. They will come, either immediately or later, when you least expect them. If you don't get an answer, you might be asking the wrong question; or, more likely, you already know the answer and need to decide to act on your truth.

You can accelerate your ascension process by the practice of accessing your Inner Wisdom in all of your chakras. Begin with your heart, and once you are proficient at finding and holding the focus of Inner Wisdom there, try doing so in your navel chakra. Once you become confident there, try your root chakra and so forth, gradually over time learning to hold the focus of Inner Wisdom in all of your chakras.

Candle Meditation for Finding Your Inner Wisdom

Another way to access your Inner Wisdom is to practice this meditation:

-   Light a white candle and invite the flame to bring to focus the pure energy of unconditional love from the Essence of Truth of the One Source of Life.
-   Sit quietly with that light and allow it to mirror the light within your new world heart chakra in the middle of your chest. This is a focus of your Inner Wisdom, your unique Essence of Truth, which is part of the One.
-   Breathe and relax into that inner light, and allow it to grow and fill your whole being. Imagine this light going with you throughout your days and nights, carrying your inner truth to support, inspire, guide, and protect you always.

Inner Wisdom and Balance Point

Once you are practiced at living from your Inner Wisdom, you can expand this focus of truth through a tool called the Balance Point, which is a second focus of Inner Wisdom, created by your Inner Wisdom. It may be placed anywhere within your aura, but it is often situated just behind your waist, within your pranic tube.

- Breathe into your body and give yourself an inner hug, all the way down to your toes and up to the top of your head, as though you are hugging someone very precious.

- Breathe into your new world heart chakra, which is in the same physical place as your old heart chakra, just a higher vibration. Allow yourself to step back into yourself, following your heart chakra backward until you are centered behind your spine. Here you will feel the energy open up into the pranic tube, where there will be a sense of peace and expansion and light. Here is the place where you may most easily access your Inner Wisdom.

- Centering on this peaceful place within, let your consciousness come to focus there, rather than in your head, as though you were looking out at the world with eyes and senses in your heart. Invite your Inner Wisdom to be in the driver's seat of your energies, rather than your head being in charge. Relax into this, and allow your Inner Wisdom to expand and fill you.

- Ask your inner wisdom, which knows how to do everything, to create a second focus of Inner Wisdom as a Balance Point. I recommend you start by asking for it about two inches in back of your waist, within your pranic tube. If that doesn't feel good, however, you may ask your Inner Wisdom to place it in the right place for you.

- Allow your focus to follow your Inner Wisdom as it establishes the Balance Point. Let yourself feel centered on your Inner Wisdom in both the Balance Point and the heart chakra. Invite the energy of both to expand and fill you.

- Each focus of your Inner Wisdom accesses pure energy from the true source of life from below you and above you through your pranic tube. Another term for this source is the Essence of Truth of God. When you access your Inner Wisdom and balance point, welcome the energy of the true source from below and above to support you with clean energy for your life.
- Practice living from your Inner Wisdom and Balance Point, for greater wisdom, stability, balance, and energy. You will discover yourself to be stronger and more effective, and things will manifest better with this grounding focus and support.

Live Increasingly in Your New World Self

During the transition to the new world energies, you have two versions of yourself—the old world self and the new world self. You will tend to flip between these different focuses. The more you live in the enlightened and harmonious new world energies, the smoother your ascension will be. The old world energies will feel by contrast darker and more uncomfortable when you slip back into that vibration. Retuning to your new world focus will make all the difference in your experience. It's almost like night and day. Don't fight with the old; live in the new, and let the old pass away from lack of energy!

The first thing you can do to live increasingly in your new world self is to center within your Inner Wisdom and ask to be focused in your new world self. When done correctly, this should give you an instant shift into a lighter and easier experience.

The Healing Qabalah Tools

The Healing Qabalah I describe here is what Archangel Michael taught me. It is simple and effective. I know many powerful ways to work with the Qabalah, but this basic method is easily learned within this context. The Qabalah is so complex that it can become the study of a lifetime if you are so inclined.

My goal here is to help you work through your Inner Wisdom to access the Essence of Truth of each sphere on your Tree of Life and its corresponding archangel. Then I will invite you to work with each archangel to tune and heal the aspects of soul associated with each sphere of your tree. Last, I will invite you to work with the archangels to help you balance and integrate the many aspects of your Tree of Life.

Archangels are God's managers. They coordinate the power and life force of the universe and the wide variety of angels who work together to give birth to the spiritual and physical world. They are beings of unconditional love who act within the creation like God's own hands, always in harmony with God's intentions.

Each sphere on the Qabalah has an archangel that oversees the energy in that aspect of creation. I will introduce you to the archangel that works with each sphere and teach you to access their energy for your healing and ascension.

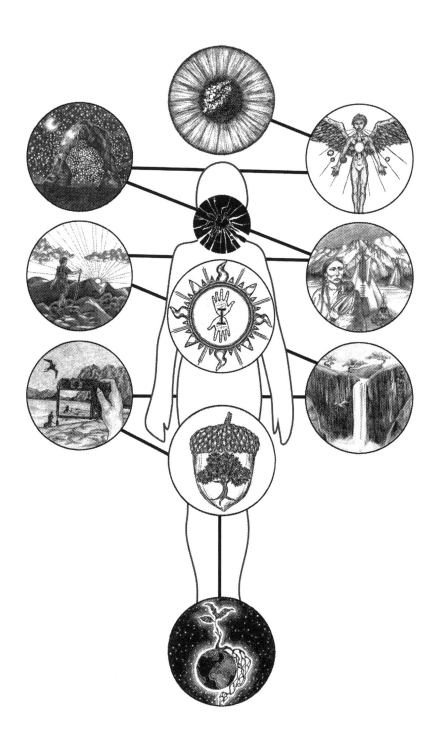

Tree of Life
As though you are looking in a mirror

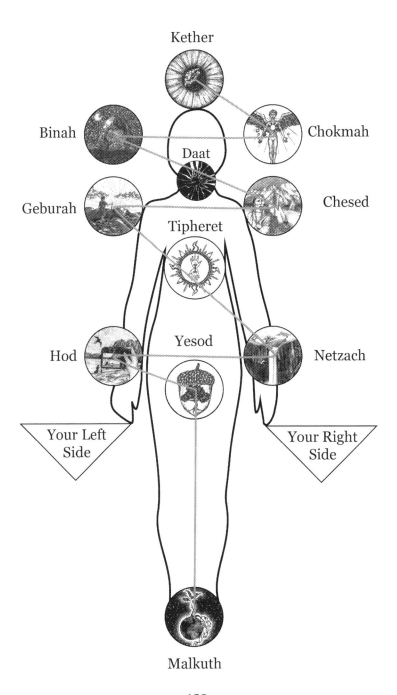

Kether

Binah

Chokmah

Daat

Geburah

Chesed

Tipheret

Hod

Yesod

Netzach

Your Left
Side

Your Right
Side

Malkuth

Healing Qabalah for Riding the Wave of Change

Look at the Qabalah diagram as though you are looking in a mirror. The spheres on your left correspond to the left side of your body and the spheres on the right correspond to the right side of your body, exactly as if you are looking at a reflection of yourself.

This is the way the Jewish Qabalah envisions the Tree of Life. Other traditions orient you as though you are backing into the Tree of Life, which can be confusing. While my work is nontraditional, I use the traditional Jewish orientation. If you have learned it the other way, you can translate the meditations to your usual orientation or try them this way. Both work! Use the Qabalah diagram as needed to guide you in the following meditations.

There are many aspects of true function within each sphere on the Tree of Life. In the following meditations, I will use those I perceive as most likely to be effective for ascension for the most people. If you would like to experience a more comprehensive study of Qabalah as a personal path for spiritual evolution, I recommend Rabbi Yonnasan Gershom's *49 Gates of Light.* (You also can find him on Facebook!) While I'm sure he wouldn't think my work traditional enough, I find his work to be very insightful—although some elements are too traditional for me. I also teach a more comprehensive Healing Qabalah in some of my courses that are described on my website!

You may do the meditation for each sphere individually, or you can do the whole series of meditations in one sitting. Alternately, you could take any pair of the spheres on opposite sides of the Tree and work their meditations together in relationship with

Tipheret, the center sphere, to increase the balance, integration, and self-mastery of those aspects of yourself. Tipheret is the point of balance, integration, and mastery of the whole Tree of Life, like the palm of the hand integrates the actions of the fingers.

Just a reminder that within each sphere on the Qabalah Tree of Life there is a whole Tree of Life; and each of those spheres also contains a whole Tree – and so on, endlessly. That is why in the meditations we ask that the spheres within the spheres be healed too.

To prepare yourself conceptually for the meditations, read the appropriate sections about the Qabalah in Part II.

Qabalah Ascension Meditations

Begin each meditation by centering on your Inner Wisdom. Add the Balance Point if you feel comfortable doing so. Stay centered in these focuses of truth within your body and soul as you use the meditations below. This will keep you grounded, so that the healing can manifest into reality for you. At the end of the meditations, follow the return to ordinary focus process provided. This deeper grounding will allow the healing work to complete over time.

If you have trouble staying focused while meditating, try doing the meditations while standing, walking, or using a treadmill or other walking-type exercise machine. The more grounded you are, the better these will work.

As you read the meditations below, allow the true vibrations of each sphere and its archangel to tune and harmonize you, bringing healing as well as helping you ascend.

To work from your Inner Wisdom and make the clearest connections to the essence of truth, I recommend that you say the meditations silently at a moderate pace, as though you were speaking from within your heart chakra and Balance Point. If you say them aloud, speak the same way, as though your voice came from there. Let the energy move through your Inner Wisdom, which will bring all your gifts to an optimal focus. Letting the energies be directed from there rather than with your head or third eye chakra, your Inner Wisdom can integrate the gifts of your head and third eye into the wholeness of your experience for great results.

Working this way, you will stay strong within yourself as you access the archangels and receive their support. You will partner with them from your strength, which allows you to grow stronger and lets them help you more.

I have written out the meditations following the order of the Path of the Lightning Bolt in the traditional way from Kether down to Malkuth. Sometimes it works better to begin in Tipheret to establish your center and open your heart to a clear focus, and then work from Malkuth up to Kether; it can help you to stay more grounded in your body, so change can happen more efficiently. You can alternate these two approaches and see which you like best.

Kether – (KET- air) Meditation – above the crown of your head

I welcome the essence of truth of Kether, Kether, Kether, One Source of Life—and the essence of truth of Archangel Metatron, Archangel Metatron, Archangel Metatron. Please tune and heal the sphere of Kether above my head and all it represents within my soul. Let the river of ascension flow from the One Source into my entire being. Awaken wholeness and my new world self within each aspect of me. Let this happen gently but powerfully with each passing day, at exactly the right pace for me. Let this river of unconditional love and healing, which flows through all creation, awaken within my being the essence of truth of me, releasing the old world illusions and the misery that went with them to be washed away. Let my old world experience dissolve gently as my new world self arises within me. Let the house of my being become a home for my eternal facet of the One True Source, to live and act within the world. Let this occur within Kether in each sphere of my Qabalah Tree of Life.

Chokmah – (Hoke-mah) Meditation – right side of your head

I welcome the essence of truth of Chokmah, Chokmah, Chokmah, Father God, unity and Cosmic Christ—and the essence of truth of Archangel Ratziel (ROT-zeel), Archangel Ratziel, Archangel Ratziel. Please tune and heal the sphere of Chokmah on the right side of my head and all it represents within my soul. First individual Being, who is the seed of independent being within all of creation, please awaken my memory of unity with the One Source and all of life. Heal the wounds of separation through unconditional love, grace, and forgiveness. Help me to see the true purpose behind all circumstances, forgive all traumas I have experienced, and claim the power and gifts I have gained through them. Assist me to reclaim my birthright as an individual aspect of the One Source, innocent, wise, and free. Let this occur within Chokmah in each sphere of my Qabalah Tree of Life.

Binah-(BEE-nah) Meditation – left side of your head

I welcome the essence of truth of Binah, Binah, Binah, beloved Mother God, Cosmic Womb; and the essence of truth of Archangel Tzaphkiel (ZAF-keel), Archangel Tzaphkiel, Archangel Tzaphkiel. Please tune and heal the sphere of Binah on the left side of my head and all it represents within my soul. Thank you for healing the trauma of separation my soul has experienced since individuating out of Oneness. Help me to reclaim my true spiritual essence and gifts of wholeness, now that I have learned to be an independent being. Remind me of the potent love that caused me to separate out of unity in order to develop my own unique facet of the One Source. Let me return to wholeness and unity while maintaining my unique focus of true self. Forgive me for all negativity through all lifetimes, and help me forgive the suffering this journey has caused myself and others. Help me to be reborn now into the new world, and to actualize my true purpose as an individual focus of the One True Source of Life within all creation. I ask that this rebirth be as gentle as is optimal for myself and for all of life. Let this occur for Binah within each sphere of my Qabalah Tree of Life.

Daat-(Dot) Meditation – back of the throat and neck
– Not a sphere, a tear in the fabric of creation

I welcome the essence of truth of Archangel Liestrom (LEE-strum), Archangel Liestrom, Archangel Liestrom. Please heal the tear that is called Daat (Dot), which has maintained separation from the One Source of Life. Heal it within every aspect of my being and every sphere of my Qabalah Tree of Life. Let it be knitted back into wholeness through unconditional love and the

Holy Spirit in the optimal way and time for me. As this primal wound is healed, let me be restored to unity, to reclaim my oneness with the Source and all of life, even while remaining an individual being. Let my soul remember that it was my choice to journey into individuality, and that I am a facet of God—not a victim of anything or anyone but a whole and unconditionally loving Being. Help me recall that the truth of who I am is, has always been, and will always be safe, eternal, and unbreakable. Let this healing occur for Daat in each sphere of my Qabalah Tree of Life.

Chesed-(KHEH-sed) Meditation – your right shoulder area

I welcome the essence of truth of Chesed, Chesed, Chesed, security, prosperity, relationships; and the essence of truth of Archangel Tzadkiel (ZAD-keel), Archangel Tzadkiel, Archangel Tzadkiel. Please tune and heal the sphere of Chesed on my right shoulder and all it represents within my soul. Help me to feel at home in the world, to find security through unity with my own facet of the One Source. Let this eternal love that gave birth to me guide and provide for me during this time of great transition within my soul and on planet Earth. Help me to let go of old habits that have limited me in body, emotion, mind, or spirit—especially unfulfilling or self-damaging relationships with people, money, food, or substances. Help me realize my true source of nourishment and provision, through the wellspring of life and love within my true self, and within the world. Let that wellspring rise through all the aspects of my life and help me ascend into my new world experience a little more each day. Whatever I do for prosperity, let me know that my employer and true provider is in fact always the One Source in Spirit, which created me and all of life. Help me remember, as I ascend into the new world, that I am not limited by the apparent sources of provision the world offers. As I do my part, living from love and truth as much as I can, in whatever field I am called to work, The One will provide whatever else is needed as I am open to receive it. Let me experience this through Chesed within each sphere of my Qabalah Tree of Life.

Geburah-(Ge-Boo-rah) Meditation – your left shoulder

I welcome the essence of truth of Geburah, Geburah, Geburah, change, discernment, assertiveness; and the essence of truth of Archangel Khamael (KA-mail), Archangel Khamael, Archangel Khamael. Please tune and heal the sphere of Geburah on my left shoulder and all it represents within my soul. Awaken the strength within me to follow my own true path moment by moment and find my unique place within the wholeness of life. Help me to discern what is true and right for me in each circumstance, to believe in and pay attention to my inner true self. Let my love for others be balanced by my love for my own unique facet of God and the purposes that only I can fulfill in this lifetime. Help me to walk my true path while accepting and encouraging others on their path, because each of us compliments each other. Help me to hold firm boundaries from a place of confidence and love, protecting where needed, and being open and trusting where appropriate. Let me release jealousy, fear, and judgmental attitudes, to discern the true value and purpose within all opportunities. Let this occur for Geburah within each sphere of my Qabalah Tree of Life.

Tipheret – (tee-Feh-ret) Meditation – center torso, heart, solar plexus

I welcome the essence of truth of Tipheret, Tipheret, Tipheret, Inner Wisdom, balance, unity, and the essence of truth of Archangel Michael, Archangel Michael, Archangel Michael. Please tune and heal the sphere of Tipheret in my heart and solar plexus and all it represents within my soul. Here within Tipheret help me find my strong focus of Inner Wisdom and become increasingly self-aware, inspired to express the essence of truth of myself in just the right ways for each circumstance of my life. Help me access each aspect of my Qabalah Tree of Life and bring them all into balance and unity of purpose. Like the palm of the hand directs the actions of the fingers, so may my Inner Wisdom direct my life through Tipheret. I ask that the river of ascension which flows from the heart of God would help me to release my old world identity and fears, and to awaken to each new level of truth I am destined for as I ascend. Help my true, new world self be born a little bit more every day. Assist me to accept, forgive, and love my human self, while I increasingly identify with my individual facet of the One Source. Help me to live from my inner truth moment by moment. Let this occur for Tipheret within each sphere of my Qabalah Tree of Life.

Netzach – (Net-zakh) Meditation – your right hip and groin area

I welcome the essence of truth of Netzach, Netzach, Netzach, the force of nature; and the essence of truth of Archangel Haniel (Ha-NEE-el), Archangel Haniel, Archangel Haniel. Please tune and heal the sphere of Netzach in my right hip and all it represents within my soul. I welcome this focus of the force of nature within me to strengthen the aliveness, passion, creative energy, and spirit of fun within my life. I ask for healing of this part of my being, which may have been overwhelmed by the judgments and agendas of my mind, other people, and circumstances. Help me to love and own this part of me, to access its fresh and magical gifts and master its challenges. Where my feelings tend to get negative or draw me into self-destructive behaviors, help me to choose to integrate and use this power within me in creative, meaningful, and life-enriching ways. I welcome the river of ascension that flows from the heart of God in unconditional love and grace, to help wash away the negativity of my past. Help me to listen to the wisdom and creative impulse of my Netzach, and through the presence of my Inner Wisdom to incorporate it into my life in optimal ways. Help my Netzach to work in harmony with my mind and Inner Wisdom, so that my creative will and instincts can be grounded and focused, to bear positive fruit in my life and actions. Let this occur for Netzach within each sphere of my Qabalah Tree of Life.

Hod – (HODE) Meditation – your left hip and groin area

I welcome the essence of truth of Hod, Hod, Hod, left brain, focus, and the essence of truth of Archangel Raphael, Archangel Raphael, Archangel Raphael. Please tune and heal the sphere of Hod on my left hip and all it represents within my soul. I ask that my mind might ascend and be illuminated, filled with the essence of truth of my own facet of the One. I ask that all untrue beliefs that have existed in my old world mind might be released over time, and to allow my truth to increasingly find focus in all my actions and thoughts. I invite the essence of truth of my Inner Wisdom to harness my gifts of mind in harmony with my feelings, instincts, Higher Self and all other aspects of my Being. Let Hod bring to focus in my life what is optimal in each moment. Where my mind is negative or stuck in old judgments and limitations, I ask that the unconditionally loving river of ascension would enfold and resolve that negativity, allowing love and truth to direct my life. Let this occur for Hod within each sphere of my Qabalah Tree of Life.

Yesod – (yeh-SODE) Meditation – reproductive area

I welcome the essence of truth of Yesod, Yesod, Yesod, unconscious beliefs, heredity and soul contracts, the seeds of my experience, and the essence of truth of Archangel Gabriel, Archangel Gabriel, Archangel Gabriel. Please tune and heal the sphere of Yesod in my reproductive area and all it represents within my soul. I ask that the unconditionally loving river of ascension, flowing from the heart of the One, would wash through my Yesod. I ask it to ascend my contracts, beliefs, assumptions, and hereditary programming increasingly into harmony with my new world truth. Where I no longer need to be limited, frustrated, or hurt by life in order to evolve, I ask that old contracts would be rewritten to reflect my soul's new world purposes. I ask for wisdom and insight to come at just the right pace, to help me finish any necessary karmic lessons, and ascend gently into my new world experience. I ask for forgiveness and healing for myself and others where that is needed. I invite the essence of truth of my own facet of God to increasingly live within my Yesod, and be born into every aspect of my life in the right way and time for me. Let this occur for Yesod within each sphere of my Qabalah Tree of Life.

Malkuth – (mal-KOOT) Meditation – your root chakra and below feet

I welcome the essence of truth of Malkuth, Malkuth, Malkuth, the physical world, and the essence of truth of Archangel Sandalphon (Sandal-phone), Archangel Sandalphon, Archangel Sandalphon. Please tune and heal the sphere of Malkuth in my root chakra and below my feet, and all it represents within my soul. I thank you Mother Earth for birthing into existence the seeds of my experience that are planted into the world from my Yesod. I ask that the river of ascension, which flows from the unconditionally loving heart of God, might remove from my world all the old world seeds and their products that are no longer reflecting what is necessary and helpful for my life. Please heal the effects of those things, both within me and in my relationships and experiences. Thank you, Mother Earth, for receiving into your fertile and loving Being, the new world seeds that are ready to recreate my experience. Nurture them so that when they grow I will be able to see myself in new ways, and understand my purpose in the world more clearly. Help me to increasingly live and work in unconditional love, truth, confidence, and pleasure. Let this occur for Malkuth within each sphere of my Qabalah Tree of Life.

Please follow the instructions on the next page to complete your meditation.

All Spheres and Archangels – wrapping up your healing work

I ask that all the Archangels would work together to complete this healing gently and effectively, in the right way and time for me. Please work through Tipheret to integrate and balance all aspects of my Qabalah Tree of Life. As I breathe into Tipheret in my heart and solar plexus chakras, I center within my wholeness. I welcome the Essence of Truth of my Inner Wisdom to direct my life in harmony with the greater good in all ways.

Thank you, Archangels! I release you now to your optimal relationship to me for ordinary things, asking that you clear whatever needs to be cleared as you go. I know you are always close at hand, but I release you out of my personal energy field so that my own true facet of The One may become sovereign within my body and aura.

Return to Ordinary Focus after Meditative Healing Work! :

Breathe into your Inner Wisdom within your heart chakra and refocus there and through your balance point. From your Inner Wisdom, ask that all your energies, including chakras, intuitive gifts and senses, body, and aura would be brought back to focus in the present time and place (name these) within yourself (name yourself). Ask to be rebalanced for whatever you need to do next.

Take time to stretch, have some water, eat something if needed, and do whatever you need to feel fully back in the present in your body and ready to do what is next in your day. Make sure you are fully grounded before you attempt to drive, cook, or do any other activity.

Owning Your Authority in Life

Ascending has to do with spiritual growth as well as evolution of life. As we ascend, we outgrow spiritual tools and ways of doing things that were once necessary and helpful but are no longer needed. Each time we shed something we have outgrown and shift into a deeper focus of self, we gain more authority over our lives. We will outgrow many things during this process, and there are a couple of ways to go about that. One is to wait until you just can't stand not to change, because it becomes obvious that the old way is not working anymore. The other is to sense the need for change and make it, like catching the crest of a wave and riding it smoothly onto shore. The second way involves trusting your Inner Wisdom about what is needed and moving with what feels right, often before you see it happening with others. Both ways will eventually result in your ascension, but the second way is less bumpy and is actually an act of leadership that requires self-confidence and courage (very Geburah).

One of the spiritual tools that some of us are outgrowing is mediumship, sometimes called channeling—but the type of channeling where a person allows another spirit to speak or act through him or her. This very valuable tool has allowed us to connect with higher wisdom during the old world state, when we couldn't connect through our personal mind and heart, chakras and aura. As healers and ascension workers, a number of us have been guided to let go of this tool that has been a gift in our past. We haven't given up communicating with our true friends in spirit, but we are doing so in a newly empowered way. The shift I am going to talk about in this chapter has allowed us to use and strengthen our personal gifts of telepathy, spiritual discernment, and our direct connection to the Essence of Truth of our Inner Wisdom and the One Source.

If you are someone who often feels spacey or ungrounded, tends to be receptive to other people's energy or environmental toxins, are easily drained or are very sensitive, the following information may be helpful to you, even if you have never thought of yourself as a medium or channel.

Gradually it came to the attention of my closest group of ascension worker /planetary healers and me that it was time for us to claim our personal authority as a facet of the One. We were guided to own our unique perspective and wisdom rather than always seeking guidance and direction from outside sources, whether those sources were in spirit or other human beings. Over time we became more like colleagues or partners to all intelligent and unconditionally loving spirit beings, teachers and mentors, rather than followers or supplicants. We learned to first seek wisdom from our Inner Wisdom and Higher Self, intuition, and instinct, and then confer with others as needed. We have been learning to identify more fully with our own Higher Self and to work directly with The Essence of Truth of God as cocreators. This change led to the release of the energy equipment that allowed us to be used as mediums. Doing so has been a surprisingly seamless transition, having no negative effect on our spiritual work at all.

Mediumship channels are openings in a soul's aura and body that allow other spirits to speak through them and sometimes act as well. This system was constructed long ago in some of the earliest civilizations on Earth to help people communicate with the spirits. Since the mid-1800s when Spiritualism began to encourage people to utilize their gifts as mediums and channels, there has been an increase in this ancient practice. It has been helpful and has had a significant impact on encouraging our awakening consciousness and ascension.

This practice was needed because our ability to communicate with those beyond the physical was very limited earlier in our evolution. Mediumship provided people with openings or channels within their energy field through which spirit might speak for reassurance and guidance. During the New Age movement that began in the 1970s and gained more influence in subsequent years, this practice became even more common and accepted. People felt empowered that they could communicate with spirit guides, and it opened a lot of doors in spiritual awareness overall.

Mediumship, however, is both empowering and disempowering. The channels create openings in a medium's energy field that allow spirits to enter and use the person's body and aura to influence the medium and others through them. These channels create blocks within the medium's energy, however, because they take up room that would ordinarily be available for a person's own use. I use the analogy of having PVC pipes running through the living space of your house. The owner of the house can't live in those spaces and has to work around them, but they hear other voices and people within them, and their energy vibrations influence the energy of the house. Some people have trouble controlling who and what uses the channels, and they begin to feel imposed on and disempowered by these visitors. Channels that are not fully protected can collect energies from other people and circumstances, making the medium absorbent and vulnerable.

If you are a natural medium or channel—whether trained or untrained—even if you are not conscious of your gift, you will know if and when it is time to make this shift. Those of us who have done so have found it to be a great relief.

Releasing these channels out of our energy fields restored peace and quiet. We were able to tune in and hear our own higher selves and Inner Wisdom more clearly. We are still able to work and communicate with other souls and spirits and with the Essence of Truth of God, but we remain grounded within ourselves and grow stronger and learn more fully from these interactions. We use our own abilities more and learn to trust ourselves increasingly. We have found it easier to ground and to focus in the world and keep our energy intact and clear. We feel calmer and more whole, and our physical bodies have become stronger and healthier as well.

As we ascend to the new world, most people will outgrow these channels and begin to directly communicate with spirit through their own energies, ultimately becoming sovereign authorities in their own lives. They will begin communicating telepathically with God and as colleagues with spirit friends and helpers. People will realize that they don't need to depend on someone else to tell them what to do, but can access their Inner Wisdom, their own true facet of God, and make choices that empower them to use their own gifts. In this way they will discover their own true purpose and fulfill their unique role as a part of the larger focus of life. This will occur naturally, whether or not the channels are removed. Removing them speeds and smooths the process for those who feel that would help.

When you feel ready to release the mediumship channels, you can do so in stages, checking to see what feels good and right to you by following the instructions below. You probably can't release them all at once, but this will create an empowered time of transition for you. Doing the other exercises in this book to strengthen your Inner Wisdom and your true connection with the One Source will help prepare you for clearing the channels, if it is what you want.

Being a medium or channel is an ancient and valid practice, and if you feel guided to maintain your channels, then I recommend that you do so and respect that choice. The following healing tool is for those who feel that they are ready to release them. If you release some and decide you want them back, you can work through your Inner Wisdom and the Essence of Truth of God to ask for that. You also have many seed-like potential channels that will open up to be used if you clear some and then want to channel again.

Clearing Mediumship Channels – how to do it when you are ready

Begin with the exercises for Inner Wisdom and Balance Point.

From your Inner Wisdom and Balance Point, invite the Essence of Truth of God and the Essence of Truth of Archangels Michael and Gabriel to take authority over the mediumship channels and those spiritual energies that have used them. Ask for the release or the rewriting of contracts with those spirits, and ask for their removal and for the removal of the channels in the right way and at the right time. Ask that any negative energies would be rendered harmless as these clear. Ask that all versions and backup systems be cleared as they become available.

From within your Inner Wisdom and Balance Point, claim that your body and aura are your own sovereign home in this world.

Most natural mediums have many channels that can be accessed from all directions through their energy fields and bodies. Work first on clearing those that are most frequently in use; then gradually, over a period of weeks or months, ask for clearing of those throughout your body and aura, working your way through and around your whole energy field. You may need to do this multiple times as you grow stronger in owning your own authority and wholeness.

Ascension Support Classes

You can experience my ascension support classes in two ways: at four-week intervals in a series of six classes or as single events for groups. These are potent, transformational, gentle, meditative group healing and ascension sessions. They assist people to let go of the old world and live more fully in the new. Each class is unique and very effective, stimulating changes that integrate smoothly and naturally for each person, as they are ready for them. Class is designed for those who will be attending, and it works through them to assist others in their soul group and throughout the world as they too are ready to ascend. Classes include a teaching period, question and answer, and sharing as well. People participate live by phone, Skype, or in person. Visit my website for the next series of monthly ascension classes or to inquire about setting up an individual ascension class for your group - www.spiritualhealers.com

The Weekly Word for Healing and Ascension

A blog every Friday will help support your journey of ascension! Keep up on what is current with ascension, including progress we are making personally and planet-wide on our road to ascension; receive meditations, reminders, and tools for your own journey! Visit www.spiritualhealers.com and click the link to the blog site. Better yet, sign up for emails and receive a blog alert every Friday morning and afternoon with a link!

Closing Thoughts

We are standing on the threshold of the new world. On one side of that threshold is the old world, with all its complexity and challenges—beautiful and terrible, and in the process of passing away. On the other side is the new world, in the process of being born. In the new world experience we will discover increasingly what it means to live from unconditional love, what it feels like to be whole, and how all our experiences will work together to create harmony with all of life.

Every one of us is a unique facet of the creative Oneness that we call God. Where our old world self and new world self rub together, it creates stress during the ascension process. This can be a reminder to invite our Inner Wisdom to take the lead through that aspect of our lives, be it spirituality or to do with physical health, emotions, mind, work, or relationships. When we do, it will help us grow and discover a new way to be in the world, by increasing our wholeness.

We have eternity to realize our full potential, which is beyond what we can conceive at this time; ascension is an ongoing journey of life. As we grow increasingly centered on our truth, we can enjoy the journey more and ride the waves of change with grace and ease!

Thank you for reading this book and riding the wave of change with me. I wish you joy and a smooth journey into the new world experience!
Visit my website for classes, workshops, healing and Ascension treatments, and to receive *The Weekly Word for Healing and Ascension*, to support your journey of change: www.spiritualhealers.com
Love and Blessings, Eve Wilson

Acknowledgments

Special thanks to Kara Bradley for her gorgeous Qabalah sphere drawings - original to this book, to Michael Brewer for his beautiful and insightful translation of the Calendar of the Soul, to Joyce Thomas for improving on my hand-drawn diagrams and cover design and art, to Anne Adamus for her generous contribution of time, skill and wisdom, to Kathleen Hallberg, Penny Golden, Richard Jelusich and Annette Aben for reading, reviewing and making very insightful suggestions, to my husband Dave for his generous help, trust and love, to Mike, Karen, Kitty and Kathleen for sharing this wild and wonderful ascension journey and for your powerful and loving support, and to all of you who have waited patiently (or impatiently) for this book to be born! Thanks also to Balboa Press for their inestimable help.

Glossary of Terms

Angels – pure spiritual beings in service to the Essence of Truth of God, as though they are God's hands; there is an angel for every created individual thing.

Archangels – pure spiritual beings, God's managers; this group and a handful of others coordinate our universe.

Ascended Masters – beings of unconditional love; those who have gone through the incarnation process and regained their unity with God while remaining individual. They can be all places at once while still maintaining their own wholeness, individuality, and unity with God and all life.

Ascension – personal and planetary; the process of all the diverse aspects of creation rising in vibration and consciousness to regain unity with God, while retaining our identity as individual souls and life forms. Our current phase of evolution on planet Earth.

Ascension Timer – the inner alarm clock that calls souls to awaken and ascend back into unity with our true spiritual source.

Belly Feelings – The intuitive gut sense of what is true and what is not.

Binah – third sphere on the Qabalah – Mother God, left side of the head, transition point between unity with Source and the journey of incarnating. The cosmic womb; restriction, understanding, faith.

Calendar of the Soul – by Rudolf Steiner, English translation by Michael Brewer © 1982, and the *Rudolf Steiner-Nachlassverwaltung*, Dornach, Switzerland.

Chesed – fourth sphere of the Qabalah – right shoulder, where we are born into family and society; where we experience love and support or their lack; where we learn to fit in or don't.

Chokmah – second sphere of the Qabalah – Father God, right side of head, the first created being individual from the One Source. Unity, wisdom, unconditional love, Cosmic Christ.

Christ – individual soul in a state of unity with God, also called Ascended Mastery. There are billions of Christ Beings in the cosmos. All beings will ultimately achieve this state. It is also the first being that was conceived out of the One, which we call the Cosmic Christ. Some religions have tried to limit this term to those who are of their faith; however, it can't be limited that way. You may use a different term for this level of being.

Christ Consciousness – the consciousness of one in the state of unity with God and all of life, not determined by religious belief.

Cocreating with God – as souls ascend into increasing unity with their own facet of the One that we may call the Essence of Truth of God, that One partners with the human facility to create our experience.

Consensual Reality - our agreed upon perception of life and truth. The way we see things collectively. Our group assumptions about reality. In the new world experience, we each create our own experience, and we no longer expect consensual reality. It never really was consensual anyway, so we just let go of that expectation, and the judgments of right and wrong that go with it.

Contracts – here we are referring to spiritual contracts or agreements that define our experience of life. These include contracts made in the material world but with a spiritual element, such as marriages, religious affiliations, promises made, etc. It also refers to the hereditary agreements and choices we enter into when we are born through two people into our physical incarnation, and the contracts that we carry through more than one lifetime for our spiritual growth and evolution, and for the roles we will play in the lives of others and the world.

Contractual Journey – the journey of life as it plays out based on our contracts.

Cosmic Christ – I use this term for the first manifestation of individual consciousness within Chokmah, sphere two in the Qabalah, which fathered all other life forms; an eternal Being still active within creation, calling us back to unity through the process of ascension. I use this term also when referring to the Christ within all of creation, because it helps to differentiate it from religious ideologies, strengthening the reality that it exists within all created souls. You may have a different word for this.

Cosmic Womb – the mother God who births pure spirit into individual lives and forms; Binah, sphere three in the Qabalah

Daat – a tear in the Qabalah or Tree of Life, in the area of the throat on our personal tree, that occurred as we transitioned from unity into individuality. A chasm we have to cross in reclaiming our unity and Oneness with Source that tends to open when we experience intolerable fear.

Dissociate – the tendency for elements of soul to fragment off from the whole soul body during unresolvable traumas, often called inner children or soul parts; a healthy response to life's challenges; can become a problem where there is a great deal of dissociation, causing people to have difficulty staying responsive and focused in their lives, or develop split personalities.

Divine – of the original Source, unconditionally loving spirit.

Ego – a person's human identity, necessary for maintaining individual boundaries and direction; can ascend into a more enlightened state; in a wounded state can be weak or overbearing.

Essence of Truth – the highest level of truth available at the present time.

Eternal – that which lasts and continues to evolve through all lifetimes.

Eve's Healing Treatments – visit www.spiritualhealers.com to find out about these effective healing and ascension treatments for body, emotion, mind, spirit, and soul. Available for adults, couples, children, families, and pets.

Facet of God – each individual person's unique aspect of the One that we call God.

Fish Hawk – osprey, sometimes known as the sea hawk or fish eagle; a diurnal, fish-eating bird of prey.

Flower essences – healing remedies for emotional and mental states made from distilled essence of flowers.

Forgiveness – happens when a person is ready to claim their power and heal. It is an absolute requirement as we work our way back to wholeness. As we ascend and realize we have contracted for challenges to be the oppositional force that helps us build our soul muscles, forgiveness becomes a natural step of letting go and moving on with our truth, in a state of gratitude for all that has made that possible.

Geburah – fifth Qabalah sphere – left shoulder, the force of change; the impulse to move beyond the familiar and fulfill our own inner direction and purpose; the assertiveness to stand up to the status quo and do what is right for one's self; when repressed, it becomes anger.

God – The first One from which all of creation comes, existing at the core of all creation as its true essence.

God Self – One's own unique facet of the wholeness that is God.

God Within – One's own unique facet of the wholeness that is God present within your body and soul.

Grace – forgiveness and healing that flows from the Essence of Truth of God, clearing the old and allowing the new to be born; the release from karmic conflicts, lessons, and contracts that are no longer needed as we move into the new world experience; a gift, freely given by God.

Healer & Ascension Certification Course – Legal National Certification for Healer Practitioners' see Eve Wilson's website for more information: www.spiritualhealers.com

Healer Practitioners – people who are legally certified to practice spiritual healing and counseling anywhere in the United States; certification available by taking The Healer & Ascension Certification Course and provided by The Universal Church of the Master who recognizes all spiritual paths; find out more at www.spiritualhealers.com or www.u-c-m.org

Healing Qabalah – using the Qabalah or Tree of Life for spiritual healing in the way Archangel Michael taught Eve Wilson.

Heart Chakra – a spiritual organ whose physical counterpart is the thymus gland, located in the middle of the chest; essential for healing and change, the heart chakra is the bridge that allows the physical and spiritual to interact.

High Vibration – all forms are made up of vibrating energy. The speed of that vibration defines the levels of consciousness able to function within the form; it is important that the vibration be in harmony with what is needed for that form, so too high can be chaotic, but too low tends to be negative; raising of vibration for a life form that happens in the right way and time for that form allows higher consciousness to awaken within it, so it comes into increased harmony with its true essence, purpose and God.

Higher Consciousness – levels of awareness that are in harmony with the Essence of Truth of God and functioning in unconditional love.

Higher Nature – the true, spiritual qualities of an individual.

Higher Self – the pure true essence of an individual soul, his or her eternal Being.

Hod – eighth sphere on the Qabalah or Tree of Life, left hip/groin, the mind, focus, ability to follow through.

Holographic – the entirety of a thing, all aspects, perceiving the wholeness of it.

Homeopathy – vibrational medicine, available in physical, emotional, mental, or spiritual potencies; heals things through affecting the energy field, rather than through physical chemical reaction; may work like an immunization, helping the body to fight off disease.

Human Vehicle – the physical body and aura, with all its capacities as a vehicle for the soul and eternal spirit that created it to act through.

"In pressure though hast enlarged me"– Psalms 4:1 King James Bible.

Incarnation – a spiritual being entering into a physical lifetime.

Individuation – a person being fully himself or herself, taking responsibility for his or her actions and choices, and living a life directed by his or her own motivation.

Inner Alarm clock – the wake-up call to ascend; goes off when it is time for people to awaken from the state of being entirely identified with their limited human experience, when they can remember that they are an eternal spirit that is living in a human experience, as a part of God within all of life.

Inner Universe – a place within a soul, accessible through the solar plexus where only that person and God can be; a kind of inner home for the soul.

Inner Wisdom – the focus of divine consciousness within the individual, most easily found within the heart chakra.

Internal Compass – the inner knowing of the truth, and of what the right direction to go is at any given moment.

Journey of separation – the old world journey of separating out of the Oneness of God, the building of individual soul bodies for each unique facet of that One to eventually be able to live and act through.

Kabbalistic Tree of Life Poster – Patricia Waldygo – published 1983 Samuel Weiser, Inc.

Karmic Wounds and Traumas – difficulties experienced on our old world journey of separation that help us grow needed soul muscles and qualities; suffering that helps us learn our lessons and evolve.

Keepers – hold the contracts for emotional, mental, or spiritual structures that block or use our power; part of the old world system of limitation and opposition to aid in soul development and individuation.

Kether – first sphere on the Qabalah or Tree of Life – above the crown of the head; the first focus of the One Source of All Life or God, the place in our evolution where we are all One, before separating into individuals.

Legally Incarnating Soul – each person's soul is huge, having been built through many incarnations; only a specific part of you is contracted to be incarnate in your body at the present time; there is some turnover during a lifetime, with some parts leaving and other parts joining what has already been here in the present incarnation.

Lower Consciousness – that which is not awake to its true spiritual self; may refer to the consciousness of the physical body and material life.

Lower Nature – the tendencies innate within the physical body, concerned only with survival and personal satisfaction or pleasure; or can refer to that which is dark and distorted in souls.

Lower spiritual energies – spiritual energies that are not enlightened, without higher purpose; may be negative or hurtful.

Malkuth – tenth sphere on the Qabalah or Tree of Life – below the feet; the earth, manifest material form.

Mastery – in the spiritual sense of the word, this means a soul evolving to the point of unifying with its higher consciousness and the Essence of Truth of God, so they are actively cocreating with God and serving the greater good.

Material Experience – that which pertains to physical life.

Mayan Calendar – The End of Time – The Mayan calendar ended on the last day of the year 2012. There are various interpretations of this ending, but some considered it would be the end of the world, heralding the destruction of the planet. I see this as the end of the old world contracts and the time when the new world contracts become authoritative in our world.

Microcosm – a community, place, or situation regarded as encapsulating in miniature the characteristic qualities or features of something much larger; for example a drop of water is a microcosm of a lake.

Monthly Ascension Support Class – Eve Wilson's class meeting every four weeks, smoothing people's journey of ascension; offering gentle healing and ascension meditations for clearing, upgrades of body, soul contracts, and assistance to others in family, soul group, and around the world as they are ready to ascend; runs for six months. Find out more at <u>www.spiritualhealers.com.</u>

Narcissistic – excessively preoccupied with personal adequacy, power, prestige, and vanity; unable to see other people's needs and desires due to this preoccupation; selfish.

Netzach – seventh Qabalah Sphere – right hip/groin; the force of nature, instinct, sexuality, feelings, creativity.

New World – the destination of the ascension process; a state of unity of true spirit with all creation; where the wise and eternal spirit of the One Source manifests individually within each created being. 340+ million years of increasing wholeness and unity of life.

Old World – the journey of evolution that has been happening since the beginning of creation, where individual aspects of the One Source were sent into the developing universe to build souls and bodies that would eventually become suitable vehicles, capable of actualizing the true potential of the One Source within individual lives and worlds.

Old World Blocks – systems that were developed as needed to provide the oppositional force to build soul muscles and qualities of being; like the workout gym of the evolutionary process. These would include physical, emotional, mental, and spiritual obstructions from all lifetimes that we have experienced. Also, the post-traumatic stresses we carry related to those experiences, which inhibit us from realizing certain gifts and potentials, but force us to grow elements of ourselves that we would otherwise not.

Oneness – the truth of all creation is that we are each a part of the One Source of Life. This oneness is a seed planted into all individual life forms. This oneness will awaken a state of wholeness within each individual as we ascend into the new world. One day all will return to Oneness with Source, but the ascended individual elements will still exist and be available to initiate a greater evolutionary process for the next round of creating.

Osprey - sometimes known as the sea hawk, fish eagle, or fish hawk, is a diurnal, fish-eating bird of prey.

Paradigm shifts – originally a term relating to an absolute shift in a scientific way of viewing reality; the term "paradigm shift" has found uses in other contexts, representing the notion of a major change in a certain thought-pattern—a radical change in personal beliefs, complex systems or organizations, replacing the former way of thinking or organizing with a radically different way of thinking or organizing.

Past Lives – incarnations or lives prior to the current one. All people and life forms experience multiple incarnations for the development and evolution of souls.

Path of the Lightning Bolt – the order of creation of the ten spheres on the Qabalah or Tree of Life flowing from Kether—the Source down through Malkuth—the earth.

Personal Tree of Life – Every facet of creation has its own Qabalah or Tree of Life. Your personal Tree of Life is the foundation for you in this lifetime.

Power Animal Merge – the process of integrating the energy of a power animal to strengthen the instinctual aspects of a person for healing and growth; power animals are aspects of true source coming to us in animal forms to help us learn to develop needed gifts and strengths.

Primal Wounds of Separation – when our Being first separated out of the One Source of all Being, we experienced feeling individual, alone, and afraid for the first time; our reactions to that are our primal wounds that we will need to heal as we ascend back into unity and unconditional love.

Psychic Boundaries – the proper energy space between individuals, allowing each to maintain the integrity of his or her true self.

Psychic Energy – a higher vibration of power and intention than what we express physically; invisible to normal vision and perception, it is an expression of feeling, thought, will, and soul; communicates with and impacts others who may or may not recognize it, but may react to it if they are intuitively sensitive in positive or negative ways, depending on the nature of what is being expressed or projected.

Psychotic Break – an episode of acute, temporary psychosis.

Qabalah – The underlying structure on which creation is built; all things have a Qabalah, from the smallest particle to the largest structure.

Qabalah Spheres – the ten spheres of the Qabalah make up the Tree of Life.

Rapids – river rapids - are sections of a river where the river bed has a relatively steep gradient, causing an increase in water velocity and turbulence; characterized by the river becoming shallower with some rocks exposed above the flow surface.

Rudolf Steiner – (1861–1925) was an Austrian philosopher, social reformer, architect, and esotericist; author of many writings, including *Calendar of the Soul* quoted throughout this book.

Separation – Journey of – the journey of evolution that has been happening since the beginning of creation, where individual aspects of the One Source were sent into the developing universe to build souls and bodies that would eventually become suitable vehicles, capable of realizing the true potential of the One Source within individual lives and worlds; the old world experience.

Shamanic Traditions – First-people medicine traditions from any culture.

Solar Plexus Chakra – the spiritual energy center associated with the upper abdomen.

Soul body – the spiritual vehicle for our eternal spirit to express through within the created universe; built and evolved through our incarnations to ultimately hold all the capacities needed to realize our potential as an aspect of the One manifesting through an individual life; lives within the physical body when incarnate, much larger than what lives in a single lifetime in the old world; will be more fully incarnated as we ascend.

Soul Contracts – spiritual contracts or agreements that direct our evolution and guide us to fulfill our purpose; they define much of what we will experience and do in our lives; may be specific to the current incarnation, or have been in place for multiple incarnations, or all of our incarnations; may be in place for groups of people through soul group and family associations.

Soul Development – the building of the soul body for our eternal spirit to act through in the world; development of particular traits, strengths, and gifts required for our spirit to express our potential.

Soul Muscles – strengths that our soul has or can develop that our spirit can use to act in the world.

Soul qualities – personality traits, gifts, and abilities that our soul possesses

Soul vehicles – the soul is the vehicle for our eternal spirit to live and express through, lives within the body when incarnate.

Souls – built through all our incarnations, the soul is the vehicle for our eternal spirit to live and express through. It is a spiritual body, like our physical body and aura, but at a higher level of vibration, which continues on between lifetimes. It is a huge body and only a part of it incarnates at one time; as we ascend, more of our soul lives within our physical body, so more of our spirit can express within a particular incarnation.

Source – the One Being out of which all life is born; the Essence of Truth of God.

Sovereign Being – as we ascend, one of our goals is to allow our own true spirit to become the authority within our body, soul, and aura; to be so whole that while we can feel or perceive what is going on around us and participate in it where appropriate, we maintain our own true energy, vibration, integrity, and wholeness.

Spacey – to be unfocussed and energetically dissipated.

Spiritualism – a religion that recognizes that the life of the soul continues beyond the experience of death; teaches spiritual healing; supports and trains psychic mediums for communicating with people who are no longer in physical bodies, spirit guides and angels.

Still Small Voice – the voice of intuition whether heard, or just known; subtle but true and trustworthy.

Template - a generic model or pattern from which other objects are based or derived.

The End of Time - See Mayan calendar.

The Holy Spirit – a substance of spirit that is the building material of the universe; flows directly from the One Source and contains within it the energy systems needed to generate life in harmony with God's true intentions; appears in meditation or healing when God is directing change to occur.

The One – the Source of Life, the Essence of Truth of God.

Tipheret – sixth Qabalah Sphere – heart and solar plexus region; the center of the Tree of Life where we can learn to balance and master the integrated expression of all of the spheres; the place where we find our easiest connection to our Inner Wisdom and personal aspect of Cosmic Christ.

Tree of Life – the Qabalah.

True Core Identity – who we really are, regardless of how we are experiencing ourselves in the outer sense; our eternal spiritual true self present within our human incarnation.

True Nature – what is natural to us when we are in harmony with our eternal and true spiritual self.

Unity – knowing and experiencing our right relationship with the One Source and all of life.

Upgrades – as we ascend into higher vibrations, our body, aura, soul, and contracts are upgraded to what supports our new level of being and function—like when children lose their baby teeth and the adult set comes in; these upgrades are present and available to us as we come into the right vibration to receive them.

Vibration – all life is energy moving at different vibrations; things that are very dense or hard are generally lower vibration than those that are more fluid and light. As we ascend, our bodies, auras, souls, and the planet all vibrate increasingly at the right levels to allow spirit to express more fully through them. Lower vibration doesn't mean bad; it just means more physically dense, which can be good for supporting and grounding higher spiritual energies. Often it is more the way something is in tune with its own spiritual energy or how it harmonizes with its true purpose that is important with regard to the speed of its vibration. Think of a tuning fork, which creates a vibration that makes a sound that you can then tune a guitar string to, or an instrument. We want the instruments of body, soul, and planet to be in harmony with their true spiritual source, so they can work together to recreate the world to accommodate true consciousness on all levels. If there is dissonance between how we experience ourselves and our truth, then it blocks the flow of higher purpose into our lives and world. So it is really about being in harmony and in balance, having the right range of vibrations for true spirit to express through.

Waldorf Education – is a humanistic approach to pedagogy based on the educational philosophy of the Austrian philosopher Rudolf Steiner, the founder of anthroposophy. The first Waldorf School was founded in 1919 in Stuttgart, Germany. At present there are 1,023 independent Waldorf schools, two thousand kindergartens, and 646 centers for special education located in sixty countries.

Yesod – ninth Qabalah Sphere – reproductive area; where our contracts, heredity, beliefs, and assumptions about life create the seed of our experience, which grows when planted in the earth of the tenth sphere, Malkuth. This then helps us to see and experience our selves in the way needed for us to grow.

About the Author

Eve Wilson is an exceptionally gifted intuitive spiritual healer. A UCM Healer Practitioner and teacher of planetary healing, self-healing, intuitive living and healing others since 1986; she is also an ordained minister who knows that no religion can understand the wholeness of life. Respecting all paths of personal and spiritual growth Eve doesn't let any of them define her. A life-affirming author and public speaker, she has published over 150 magazine articles on healing and spiritual living plus her empowering blog, The Weekly Word for Healing and Ascension. Eve's passion is the evolution, ascension, and healing of people and the planet. She lives in Ann Arbor, Michigan, with her husband, Dave, and their dog, Tobias where they love wildlife, the Great Lakes and the out of doors.

Riding the Wave of Change is the product of Eve's 30 year quest for the next higher perspective on life and how to heal people and the planet on the deepest levels. Where our world is struggling under the burden of climate change and human interference, Eve sees an inevitable ascension and rebirth.

Printed in the United States
By Bookmasters